Reading: A Very Short Introduction

VERY SHORT INTRODUCTIONS are for anyone wanting a stimulating and accessible way into a new subject. They are written by experts, and have been translated into more than 45 different languages.

The series began in 1995, and now covers a wide variety of topics in every discipline. The VSI library currently contains over 600 volumes—a Very Short Introduction to everything from Psychology and Philosophy of Science to American History and Relativity—and continues to grow in every subject area.

Very Short Introductions available now:

Available soon:

For more information visit our website

www.oup.com/vsi/

Belinda Jack

READING

A Very Short Introduction

OXFORD

UNIVERSITY PRESS

Great Clarendon Street, Oxford, OX2 6DP,
United Kingdom

Oxford University Press is a department of the University of Oxford.
It furthers the University's objective of excellence in research, scholarship,
and education by publishing worldwide. Oxford is a registered trade mark of
Oxford University Press in the UK and in certain other countries

© Belinda Jack 2019

The moral rights of the author have been asserted

First edition published in 2019

Impression: 1

Published in the United States of America by Oxford University Press
198 Madison Avenue, New York, NY 10016, United States of America

British Library Cataloguing in Publication Data
Data available

Library of Congress Control Number: 2018967690

ISBN 978-0-19-882058-1

Printed in Great Britain by
Ashford Colour Press Ltd, Gosport, Hampshire

For my women reader friends at
Her Majesty's Prison, Send, Surrey, UK

Contents

List of illustrations

Chapter 1
What is reading?

What do we mean by reading?

Most of us take reading for granted. It's only if we're involved in teaching someone else to read, for example, that we may realize what a strange and complex process or series of processes it is. The neurology, or neuropsychology, of reading remains a relatively primitive field of research. It's not surprising. Reading can have myriad effects on us. These can be frightening, spiritual, emotional, erotic, motivating, entertaining, informative, and enlightening—and so much more. And each of these descriptions is open to further interpretation. One person's idea of the erotic may not always match another's. The sexologist Thomas Laqueur goes as far as to argue that private reading itself made masturbation possible, irrespective of the reading material. He also argues that the stimulus of the imagination encourages self-absorption and a feeling of freedom from social constraint.

Where and with whom we read will also affect how we understand and respond to our reading. For a very long period most people were read *to*; and as children this may be our first introduction to the written word. We may read at the same time as being read to, following the text while listening to it being read. This is the case with a good deal of reading in religious settings. We read at school and university, at work, at home, while eating, while travelling, in the garden, in parks, while waiting for an appointment, on the beach, in libraries, and so on. We read alone and in more sociable spaces. We may choose to conceal what we are reading—or to flaunt it, to suggest our interests, to advertise our political or gender allegiance, our degree of education, our cultural awareness, and so on. Reading material can act as a powerful symbol. Its materiality may matter as much as its content. In the Semitic religions—Judaism, Christianity and Islam—the book may be an object of veneration or fetishism. Within numerous religious practices the book may be raised, carried in procession, kissed, and so on. At the same time, the material existence of the book may tell us relatively little about reading. Between the first publication of Mao's *Little Red Book* in 1961 and the height of the Cultural Revolution in 1969, 740 million copies may have been printed. Its cultural and symbolic value may endure however little we know about how it was and is read, and by whom.

We can read one thing at a time, or we can read multiple sources more or less simultaneously. We may think of this skipping from text to text as a new phenomenon, the 'clicking on' of the digital reading age, but libraries have long been organized to allow for the consultation of multiple volumes more or less at the same time. The bookwheel or reading wheel (see Figure 1), invented in the 16th century, was a large rotating bookstand that allowed for a variety of heavy books to be consulted easily, and for reading backwards and forwards between a number of books.

We don't read only print and its electronic facsimiles; we read landscapes, facial expressions, tea leaves, mathematical formulae, the future, and all manner of material on the internet. Mostly we think of reading as a process of decoding written and digital material and this may be as varied as a logo on a T-shirt, a poem, a political manifesto, guidebooks and handbooks (terms that suggest reading formats providing help and facility of access), tweets, graffiti, maps, a phone bill, tattoos, a dictionary, blogs, Wikipedia, crossword clues, the famously illegible doctor's

FIGVRE CLXXXVIII.

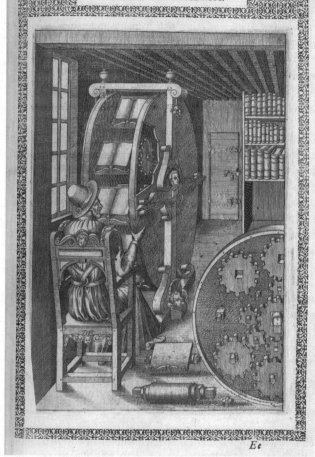

What is reading?

Ee

1. Sixteenth-century bookwheel.

prescription (now generally printed not handwritten), legislation, a till receipt, an eBook, the lists of ingredients on food packaging, or a recipe, and so on. And in the ancient world reading could be still more varied involving inscriptions on public monuments that very few could read but which everyone understood as symbolic of the power of the state. Inscriptions might not have been read in the sense we usually understand, but they had meaning for those whose eyes encountered them all the same. Ovid (43 BCE–17/18 CE) describes a love letter sent by a Roman slave. The letter had been written on his body.

Some forms of reading are both literal and metaphorical. We might read an entry in an encyclopedia but we also refer to encyclopedic knowledge, suggesting that the acquisition of literacy will give us access to all we could possibly need or want to know. This isn't, of course, the case. 'Knowing' is more than a matter of being able to read. Nor is 'literacy' an unproblematic concept. We know that during the medieval period in Europe, and at other times in other parts of the world, ideas about literacy have been very different. Lady Eleanor De Quincy was unable to write, but could read in three languages (Latin, French, and English). She commissioned the *Lambeth Apocalypse*, a highly illustrated work in the Apocalypse devotional manuscript tradition. This required both reading skills and a kind of meditative reading ability that involved keeping a holy image in the mind's eye while reading. What mattered was contemplation, the reader 'seeing with the heart'. Not dissimilarly, Buddhist texts were designed to be read, but principally in order to be memorized. The objects themselves were objects of veneration (see Figure 2).

Scholars have argued that European medieval texts were intended to be read in myriad different ways, out loud or silently, by a lone reader, or in a group, and assimilating varying degrees of meaning as a function of both word and image and in different linguistic registers. Legal documents were decorated with seals and images which had to be interpreted along with the text.

2. A Buddhist library.

We may gain a high level of literacy, as understood in the modern world, but this doesn't guarantee understanding of the written word in whatever media. Language, whether oral or written, is a slippery business and always subject to misunderstanding and misreading. Take a recipe, a piece of writing designed to be unproblematic. If the instructions that are given are not clear then the dish may be a disaster (see Figure 3).

But if basic instructions are subject to misreading or misunderstanding, then how do we make sense of idioms, metaphor, and figurative language and all those techniques that make for effective use of language, particularly the language of literature, where the highest density of ambiguous language is arguably to be found? When we read that 'All the world's a stage', we understand. But how? Literature provides the most privileged examples of the complexities of the act of reading itself.

To understand reading we need to appeal to a wide range of disciplines—myriad forms of history, literary and textual studies, psychology, phenomenology (the science of things as opposed to

5

THE RECIPE SAID "STAND FOR
FIVE MINUTES"

3. Cartoon.

the science of the nature of being), and sociology, to name the
most obvious. Historians of the book and literary scholars have
dominated research. What is now widely accepted is that reading
is far more than the decoding of messages that have been
previously encoded. The way we read is conditioned in all manner
of ways. The look of what we read already stimulates certain
expectations. Pink high-heeled shoes on the front cover of a novel
suggests that what we will read belongs to the category of 'chick lit'.
Every aspect of a text's design, whether it be in paper or electronic
form, influences how we read. These are not trivial matters.

Jan Tschichold (1902–74), author of the ground-breaking *The Form of the Book*, a study of typography, was born in Germany but in 1933 he was imprisoned by the Nazis because of their antipathy to the New Typography. To the contemporary reader, Tschichold's precepts could not be more ideologically innocent: 'The Typography of books must not advertise. If it takes on elements of advertising graphics, it abuses the sanctity of the written word by coercing it to serve the vanity of the graphic artist incapable of discharging his duty as a mere lieutenant.'

Reading is both a physical and mental activity. It stimulates neurological pathways in ways which remain to some extent a mystery, despite sophisticated methods of brain imaging. Physically, or more accurately physiologically, the eye (or finger in the case of Braille) has to 'see' (or feel), identify, and recognize the printed words. Chemical processes are then triggered which create patterns of nerve currents which are sent to the brain. The cerebral cortex interprets the data. The eyes are involved in various movements, first: fixation (the eyes dwell), then inter-fixation (the eyes move from one point of rest to another) and return sweeps (when the eye travels backwards and forwards). There may also be saccades, regression, and spans of recognition. Saccades are associated with the highly literate and involve hopping or jumping ahead of what is being read to prepare for later text-recognition. Regression requires a return to an earlier section of text to reread what may not have been fully understood—or to enjoy again. Spans of recognition are the expert reader's ability to take in large groups of words at one go. Readers of Braille engage in very similar ways with the 'reading' finger (see Figure 4).

Linguisticians and literary scholars are not the only specialists who work on reading as a subject. Psychologists and neuroscientists have also made intriguing discoveries. Psychologists have conducted extensive research into the teaching and practice of reading. What is clear is that completely to analyse what we do when we read would be the epitome of a psychologist's achievements.

4. Child reading Braille.

It would mean making sense of the most complex workings of the mind, as well as unravelling the convoluted story of the most remarkable act that civilization has learned in all its history.

Neurologists consider that they are still very much in the foothills when it comes to understanding what goes on when we read complex language but some of the initial research is intriguing. Scientists have known about 'classical' language regions in the brain like Broca's area and Wernicke's, and that these are stimulated when the brain interprets new words. But it is now clear that stories activate other areas of the brain in addition. Words like 'lavender', 'cinnamon', and 'soap' activate both language-processing areas of the brain and also those that respond to smells. Significant work has been done on how the brain responds to metaphor, for example. Participants in these studies read familiar or clichéd metaphors like 'a rough day' and these stimulated only the language-sensitive parts of the brain. The metaphor 'a liquid chocolate voice', on the other hand, stimulated areas of the brain concerned both with language—and with taste. 'A leathery face'

8

stimulated the sensory cortex. And reading an exciting, vivid action plot in a novel stimulates parts of the brain that coordinate movement. Reading powerful language, it seems, stimulates us in ways that are similar to real life.

But despite all the research in so many domains reading remains in many ways mysterious because it is often impossible to generalize, to move from the individual reading experience to a general and more theoretical model. Did the invention of printing change the reader's mental universe? There is no simple answer to the question. What we read also has a material presence and the object of what we read has multiple roles. Books have mattered for what can be read inside them but they have also mattered for the taking of oaths, as gifts, and prizes. And the bestowing of legacies which is widespread in diverse societies may be significant in very different ways. The role of books in folklore and, contrariwise, the importance of allusions to folklore in written texts demonstrates a two-way relationship between oral and written or printed material.

It is these metamorphoses and movements which make a nonsense of ideas of what we read as 'belonging' to 'world literature', or the 'post-colonial', or whatever other 'category' of writing might be proposed. Writers may be more or less sensitive to the question of their readers. The 'Nigerian' author Chimamanda Ngozi Adichie is published in the UK by Fourth Estate, in the USA by Alfred A. Knopf. In Nigeria, however, she is distributed by Muhtar Bakare Kachifo, a company conceived with the mission of 'Telling our Own Stories' (Farafina) which boasts an impressive and wide-ranging publishing list across numerous disciplines. It has its own on-line outlet, awards prizes, and publishes its own creative writing magazine, *Farafina*. To reach different readerships she is conscious of the need for multiple publishers and distributors.

Written material is wonderfully non-cognizant of physical space. It has no respect for linguistic or national borders. Their authors may or may not belong to an international republic of letters and those who make writing available to large numbers may or may not understand the language in which the text is written. Booksellers have often been itinerant—and may now be on-line—transcending national and linguistic boundaries. To think of reading in terms of an 'elite' and a 'popular' audience is no longer adequate; nor is the model of cultural change linear, or characterized by the 'trickle-down effect'. The model has to be one that allows for reversals of the current and for the muddying of the water. As historians of the book and reading have demonstrated, Gargantua (who first appeared in 16th-century French writings), Cinderella (whose origin may be in the story of Rhodopis by Strabo (*c*.7 BCE), which tells of a slave girl who marries the King of Egypt), or Buscon (who first appears in the picaresque tales of 17th-century Spain) move backwards and forwards between oral traditions, chapbooks (cheap pamphlets containing tales, ballads, or tracts and sold by pedlars), and 'sophisticated' literature, changing both nationalities and genres. The author Salman Rushdie is one of the most eloquent critics of national literatures. In his essay 'Notes on Writing and the Nation' he writes:

> Nationalism corrupts writers too...In a time of ever more narrowly defined nationalisms, of walled-in tribalisms, writers will be found uttering the war cries of their tribes...Nationalism is that 'revolt against history' which seeks to...fence in what should be frontierless. Good writing assumes a frontierless nation. Writers who serve frontiers have become border guards.

The earliest readers

Both Neanderthals and early *homo sapiens* read markings on bones although what they signified remains an unresolved question—a record of days and lunar cycles, scores of some game? The Ishango bone is a slightly curved fibula of a baboon, about 10 cm long and dark brown in colour, with a piece of quartz fitted into one end. It is named after the place where it was found, in today's Democratic Republic of Congo. It may date back as far as

22,000 years. The notches are clearly man-made—this hasn't been disputed by archaeologists. So the question is, how were these 'read' by early man? If they are 'symbols'—signs that bear no resemblance to what they represent—what do they stand for? What can this ancient piece of baboon bone tell us about the earliest 'reading'? All manner of fascinating theories have been proposed. It says something wonderful about our humanity—and fascination with reading—that a small, very old animal bone with a few markings on it can arouse such intense speculation and debate.

Among the most convincing theories are those that decipher mathematical meaning. One school of thought believes that the three columns of asymmetrically grouped notches imply that the implement was used to construct a number system and it has to be read as a numerical calculator. There have also been arguments that the bone can be read as an astronomical text, recording the lunar calendar. Microscopic imagery suggests that the notches correspond with a six-month lunar calendar. Other explanations include theories that the notches mark out stages in the female menstrual cycle.

The oldest inscribed (as opposed to carved) artefacts so far discovered are the Uruk bone tags, found in Egypt. The so-called U-j bone tags are not engraved with full writing; that is, the markings do not represent the spoken sounds of the Sumerian or Egyptian language of the 4th millennium BCE. The numbers and the pictograms showing cereal and birds, for example, can be 'read' in any language. The transformative breakthrough came with the rebus. The word derives from the Latin word meaning 'by things', 'by means of things'. The rebus allows the elements of any spoken word to be conveyed by means of signs. Thanks to the rebus, the sounds of spoken language could be systematically represented. The rebus principle has made something of a comeback in the electronic age—the text-message. It was kept alive in puzzles and by puzzle-lovers like Lewis Carroll, the author of the *Alice* books for children, *Alice's Adventures in Wonderland* and *Alice Through the Looking Glass*. Carroll would write to his young friends in rebus letters. 'Dear' would be represented by a little abstracted sketch of a deer; 'are', from the verb 'to be', would be represented simply by the letter 'r', and so on. Among the earliest ancient rebuses are Sumerian accounting tablets which date from around 3000 BCE.

This new communication system spread west to the Nile, east to the Iranian Plateau, and even to the Indus. The Sumerians lived in what is now modern Iraq. During the 3rd millennium BCE, a very intimate cultural symbiosis developed between the Sumerians and the Akkadians, which included widespread bilingualism. Gradually Akkadian replaced Sumerian, probably *c.*2000 BCE. So what is there to read in this, the oldest written language of our race? Well, a surprising amount: hymns, lamentations, prayers (to various gods), incantations (against various sources of evil), romantic literature, wisdom literature (proverbs, fables, riddles), long epics, and myths. In total some 550 'texts' exist.

One of the most famous myths, which finds its counterpart in numerous other traditions, tells of the goddess Inanna and her journey into the underworld. But much that was committed to writing is, in effect, history, records of the lives and deeds of Uruk's kings: Enmerkar, Lugalbanda and, most famously, Gilgamesh. The *Epic of Gilgamesh* exists in a number of versions but each is essentially a love story. At the same time it is an exploration of aspects of our common humanity: our propensity for egotism and the temptations of ambition. On the other hand love and friendship are celebrated and our fear of loss, and knowledge of our own mortality, are recognized. Gilgamesh himself is a compound being—part man, part god. Each version of the story has essentially the same plot. Gilgamesh must leave Uruk, undertake a quest beset by obstacles, and then return home. The plot is an archetypal one. Other oral genres which were memorialized included legal, medicinal, culinary, and astronomical writings.

Not dissimilar literary texts began to appear during the Egyptian Middle Kingdom. One outstanding feature of this early Egyptian writing was its formal poetic characteristics. They employed a particular kind of metre, with units of two or three stresses each. This is a very early example of scansion, a way of organizing writing so as to encourage a very particular way of reading it. A celebrated example is the didactic tale, 'A Dialogue of a Man with his Soul', also known as 'A Debate Between a Man tired of Life and his Soul', or 'A Dispute over Suicide' (*c.*1937–1759 BCE).

The Cretan script known as Linear A, found on Minoan tablets, dating from around 1750 BCE provides the earliest examples of European writing and remains undeciphered. The Olmec script from the Veracruz area of the Gulf of Mexico is the most ancient writing discovered from the South American region. Whether or not it is full writing remains a subject of controversy. It dates from *c.*900 BCE, at least a millennium before the Mayan scripts which are the best understood of all pre-Columbian Mesoamerican writing. There are examples carved into monumental tombs and other monuments, but also on fragments of wood, jade, and painted pottery and murals. Given the archaeological wealth and sophistication of Mayan civilization, it is quite possible that large numbers of codices (books made from hinged leaves as opposed to a scroll), made of bark paper and animal hide, have been lost. These would most likely have contained the same range of genres that existed in the ancient European centres of civilization.

Despite the innovation of full writing, most reading remained a simple activity as what was recorded was very basic information—names, numbers, and objects. Interestingly the Sumerian for 'to read', *šita*, also means 'to count, calculate, memorize, recite, read aloud'. Only a very small percentage of

the population learnt to read and it was almost exclusively a
work-related skill. Some letters, however, demonstrate that
writers and readers enjoyed poetic turns of phrase. An Egyptian
bureaucrat, writing to his son some four millennia ago, advised:
'Set your thoughts just on writings, for I have seen people saved
by their labour. Behold, there is nothing greater than writings.
They are like a boat on water...Let me usher their beauty into
your sight...There is nothing like them on earth.' Reading, by
implication, is likened to making sense of words lifted into dry dock.

The transformation of Greek orality into Greek literacy has
sometimes been described as a crisis. It was certainly a
revolutionary moment. The Greek script was phonetic and
non-standardized. They wrote *scriptio continua*, that is without
breaks between the words. This made Greek script very hard to
read. But it becomes easily comprehensible when read aloud
correctly. Reading was regarded primarily as an oral performance.
The writer's task was, in a sense, complete only when his words
had been enunciated. It has also been said that the Greeks
sometimes cast the writer and the reader as a homosexual couple
in which the reader was the passive accomplice of the writer.
Writing words was very much like writing music: both are
performative acts.

By the 3rd century BCE, in the Greek-dominated society of
Alexandria, reading and writing were part and parcel of most
aspects of commercial, political, and social life. It is no surprise,
therefore, that it was here that the first great library of the world
was founded: the Library of Alexandria. It was established by
Alexander's successor, Ptolemy I Soter, a Macedonian Greek, who
ruled 323–285 BCE. The idea of the library was the result of a
fusion of Greek and Egyptian ideals: the library would contain
the sum of human learning. And the library of one of the world's
earliest bibliophiles would eventually make its way to the Library
of Alexandria—Aristotle's private book collection. It was here that
the first complex system for indexing holdings was also invented.

The catalogue contained some 120 scrolls, listing the library's contents which exceeded some half a million scrolls.

Almost as important as the holdings themselves, in terms of understanding the scholarly mind of the time, are the sections or categories into which the catalogue was divided. There were eight classes in the library: drama, oratory, lyric poetry, legislation, medicine, history, philosophy and 'miscellaneous'. The most obvious absence was that of theology, the category which would represent virtually the entire holdings of the great medieval libraries in the West. This is evidence of two very different reading cultures. The library also housed a museum, a garden, a common dining room, a reading room, lecture theatres, and meeting rooms, a model which would become the blueprint for the great monastic foundations, colleges, and universities of Western Europe.

Western reading is a slim chapter in the history of reading until the 18th century. Most reading went on in China, Korea, Japan, the Americas, and India. It was during the Chinese Shang civilization that writing first appeared in that part of the world, and the characters are recognizable as they are very much like modern Chinese characters. The 'oracle bones', as they are known, were found in Anyang, north China, and were produced around 1200 BCE. It is possible that markings on pottery belonging to the Yang Shao culture, dating from a much earlier period, are examples of an older form of Chinese writing. While writing and reading appeared in north-central China around 1400 BCE, it was from the 5th century BCE on that writing and reading took off as something much more important than record-keeping, allowing insight into the minds of its scribes. The Chinese composed long historical and philosophical texts written with ink brushes on various supports including bark, bamboo, and strips of wood.

Before long Chinese 'literature', as it can now be termed, consisted of five books: the *Yijing* (literally 'Book of Changes'), *Shujing*

('Book of Documents', Shang and early Zhou writings (1122–256 BCE), mostly prayers and legends), *Shijing* ('Book of Songs', poetry and folksongs), *Chungqiu* (Spring and Autumn Annals), and *Liji* ('Book of Rites', a collection of texts about ritual and conduct). By the Han period (the first two centuries BCE), public libraries contained hundreds of texts written on bamboo, strips of wood, and later paper scrolls. Basic techniques of printing developed using woodblocks and it was this method that supplied readers in China, Korea, and Japan with millions of pages of reading material for the world's largest groups of readers.

The next major revolution in the history of Chinese reading was the invention of paper in 105 CE. It was this that triggered the extraordinary expansion of reading throughout East Asia. What was available to read was voluminous and varied, though much of the more literary works concerned proper conduct and correct social relations rather than something more purely imaginative or escapist. Also remarkable was the recognition that literacy was in the interests of the common good, and the education of the lower classes of society was deemed to underpin, rather than threaten, the ruling classes. But the true printing revolution came only in the 16th century and by the 17th the Chinese probably published more books than all the world's other languages together. The other part of the world with a remarkable early reading tradition was pre-Columbian Mesoamerica where there were probably some fifteen distinct writing conventions, several preserved only in a single extant inscription.

Learning to read

Reading is specific to the human species, like speech, but reading doesn't follow from innate capabilities which are activated simply by spending time with written materials. One of the most remarkable features of reading is that it has to be taught formally. Babies learn to speak by imitation and don't require any structured learning in order to assimilate grammar, syntax, and vocabulary.

This is not the case with reading, regardless of the language involved. Character-based languages (Mandarin, for example), Arabic script, Cyrillic, and Latin-based languages are taught in different ways. Without the pedagogy children, and also adults, remain illiterate. There are some 774 million, roughly 20 per cent of the global adult population, illiterate people in the world. Illiteracy is the inability to derive meaning from the linguistic symbols of a writing system. This may be the result of dyslexia, for example, a cognitive difficulty generally understood to be a neurological learning disability that impairs a person's ability to read. There are generally believed to be at least two forms of dyslexia: developmental dyslexia, which is a learning disability, and alexia or acquired dyslexia, which refers to reading difficulties that occur following brain damage, stroke, or progressive illness.

While literacy used to be understood as the ability to read and write, more recently, literacy has expanded to mean the ability to use language, numbers, and images. Literacy allows for the assimilation of useful knowledge and to communicate it. According to the *OECD*, literacy includes both the skills to access knowledge through new technologies and the ability to assess complex contexts in which knowledge may be communicated. There are levels of literacy too. The ability to speed read with high levels of comprehension remains a key skill in many walks of life.

Reading is also a highly complex activity requiring an understanding of heterogeneous linguistic phenomena, including speech sounds, spelling, and grammar. It has been argued that it is not monolithic (singular and straightforward) but rather a creative process which reflects the reader's attempt to find a particular meaning, or meanings, within the strictures of language.

Reading is the result of a slow assimilation of skills under the direction of patient teachers (see Figure 5). It begins with sounding

5. Fresco showing a child being taught to read, 1st century BCE.

words out and learning how to make sense of them, then sentences, and finally what we might call the 'global meaning' of a text. Whole-word recognition may also become a quick means of reading. The learner-reader also has to understand that a story, for example, is not simply a juxtaposition of sentences. Rather there are 'befores' and 'afters', and there are relations of cause and effect between events. Without necessarily learning formal grammar, the learner-reader of fiction has to understand that a character first introduced as Catherine is the same character referred to later on by the pronoun 'she', or the character who reappears as a definite article, followed by a noun, qualified by adjectives, 'the intelligent little girl'; 'Catherine', 'she', and 'the intelligent little girl' are all the same 'character'. As we develop as readers we need to be able to identify irony, parody, and the relationship between what we are reading and other reading material. Aimé Césaire's retelling of Shakespeare's *Tempest* needs to be read as a version of Shakespeare's play. As a West Indian writer Césaire's reading of Shakespeare is particular and our reading of Césaire will be different according to whether we know the text that Césaire is

18

writing *against*—or not. Most of what we read belongs in a particular context and this conditions—more or less—how we read.

We have some interesting insights into the history of learning to read in England. The first mention of the word 'primer', for example, is in Geoffrey Chaucer's 14th-century *Prioress's Tale*. A 7-year-old boy is in the schoolroom learning to read. Few examples of these flimsy reading primers have survived but there are some.

They were generally eight small folios in an unbound book measuring no more than a cigarette box, although much thinner. The alphabet would be at the front of the primer, then the Lord's Prayer, the Hail Mary, and finally the Creed. These were the three foundation texts of medieval English Christianity. Primers might include a number of other texts to be learnt by heart, the seven deadly sins, and the cardinal virtues for example. Thanks to primers, book-learning spread out from monasteries into people's homes allowing almost everyone to gain some degree of literacy. By 1500 writing and reading were familiar to the entire medieval population and everyone knew someone who could read.

Pedagogical controversies about how to teach reading have often become highly charged and politicized. In the USA a book entitled *What Ivan Knows That Johnny Doesn't*, published during the Cold War, demonstrated the relationship between worries about reading methods and the then fears about Soviet domination. The author, Arther Thrace, compared the advanced reading skills of Soviet schoolchildren with the very basic skills of American children of the same age.

The controversy between two reading approaches, the teaching of phonics (the 'sounding out' of units of sound in a language), versus look-say (or 'whole word recognition'), was similarly politicized in 1960s America. 'Look-say' was quickly deemed 'progressive', while phonics was associated with an upper-middle-class, college-educated 'elite'. At the same time those advocating phonics claimed that this was a matter of universal inclusion, a matter even of democracy. Gradually, amid the upheavals of the 1960s, phonics, with its emphasis on method and discipline, became symbolic of a return to law and order.

To read or not to read

Most of us assume, most of the time, that reading is synonymous with being a useful, educated citizen. And there have been myriad claims for the benefit of reading for the human mind. Anthropologists, in particular, have argued that writing imposes a particular 'logic' on human thought processes. It encourages a certain way of linear thinking and reasoning. It is commonly assumed that the advent of reading was responsible for more complex social and political structures. Administratively, comprehensive records could be kept, sophisticated communication could take place, allowing for the systematic establishment of tax systems, property rights, and other complex forms of legislation. The idea of the state as a human collective is hard to imagine in the absence of written records—and the relatively widespread ability to read. Revolutionary states in the 20th century, including the Soviet Union under Lenin and Stalin, and Mao's China, campaigned successfully to promote literacy, while trying to keep control of what was read. Lenin once said that 'Politics does not exist for someone who cannot read.'

Some anthropologists have wanted to take the argument a step further to claim that a literate person *thinks* differently from his illiterate counterpart. Reading allows for a transcendence of the self, a new sense of belonging in time and space and, most contentiously, a critical perspective on the society to which the individual belongs. Reading and writing allowed for the gradual replacement of myth, as knowledge, by science; and, equally, the replacement of accepted custom by reasoned ways of going about things.

But are these assumptions justified? Are they simply founded in Western prejudices against non-literate societies? Attitudes to reading have a history as long as the history of literacy itself. In the ancient world both Socrates (*c.*470–399 BCE) and Plato (*c.*427–347) were highly suspicious of the written word, believing that the oral tradition, in the mouths of trained intellects, maintained 'correct' interpretations. And in 5th-century Athens, there were very few books. This changed dramatically in a single generation. Aristotle amassed his own private library and was an avid reader.

In the colonial and post-colonial world the prima facie case for the merits of literacy was again challenged. Some of the arguments echoed those of Socrates and Plato. The Indian writer Ananda Coomaraswamy was one of the first, in his essay *The Bugbear of Literacy* (1947). He concludes, 'Our blind faith in literacy not only obscures...the significance of other skills, so that we care not under what subhuman conditions a man may have to earn his living, if only he can read, no matter what, in his hours of leisure; it is also one of the fundamental grounds of inter-racial prejudice and becomes a prime factor in the spiritual impoverishment of all the "backward" people whom we propose to "civilize". The idea that the acquisition of literacy skills is synonymous with the coming of 'civilization' was widespread in the European empires. When the Melbourne Public Library was opened in 1856 it represented the arrival of the civilization of the printed word in the Australian colonies of the United Kingdom. The local newspaper, *The Age*, announced a new 'epoch in our advancement', 'another stride forward in civilization'.

For the European Enlightenment philosophers of the 18th century reading was the activity that educated us out of stupidity, superstition, and barbarism, and was a precondition for modern democracies. The French *philosophes* aimed to include all human knowledge in a huge encyclopedia in the interests of education, learning, and science. The project was more than the sum of its parts, however. The point was to reconfigure man's relationship with the natural world according exclusively to reason.

The Enlightenment philosopher François-Marie Arouet, known by his nom de plume Voltaire, published his essay *On the Terrible Danger of Reading* in 1765. It is a parody of a totalitarian society in which reading has been made illegal: 'For the edification of the faithful and for the well-being of their minds, we forbid them ever to read any book, on pain of eternal damnation.' The decrees that make up Voltaire's essay, we learn at the end, have been pronounced in the 'Palace of Stupidity', in 1143. Voltaire spent much of his life in exile (or prison) because of his inflammatory ideas about politics and religion and his books were periodically banned and burned as reading them would allegedly undermine French society. An enterprising Parisian publisher even produced a fire-proof edition of Voltaire decorated with a phoenix ready to rise out of its own ashes.

In 1789, the French National Assembly issued *The Declaration of the Rights of Man and the Citizen* which included the right of any citizen to 'speak, write, print freely'. This declaration in turn influenced the Universal Declaration of Human Rights adopted by the United Nations in 1948. Interestingly, while Article 26 asserts the right to education, the Declaration makes no mention of reading or literacy. Yet in the United States the practice of reading for information, self-improvement, and civic improvement was well entrenched by the 19th century. As Protestant evangelism lost its force, reading for entertainment and aesthetic pleasure became acceptable.

The dominance of the so-called West over the rest has been put down to the word more than the sword. And the knowledge of the classical West, many would argue, was preserved thanks to the libraries of Byzantium, the Irish monks, the priests of the Roman Catholic Church, and the Muslim Abbasid caliphs (566–653 CE).

It was essentially their stewardship that allowed the civilization of the West to re-emerge in the Italian Renaissance.

Thinkers from René Descartes to John Ruskin have celebrated reading as the fundamental path to knowledge. Descartes claimed, 'Reading all the great books is like a conversation with the most honourable people of earlier centuries who were their authors', and Ruskin, similarly, argued, 'Reading is precisely a conversation with men who are both wiser and more interesting than those we might have occasion to meet ourselves.' Both these quotations are cited by Marcel Proust, in his essay *On Reading* (1905), but he contradicts the idea of reading as a conversation with the wisest. The fundamental difference between reading and conversing, according to Proust, is that reading is a solitary activity which allows the reader to maintain uninterrupted intellectual control over what is being read. Proust is interested in the interpretative dimension of reading and it is this aspect that explains why reading has always been—and remains—a potentially subversive activity.

Chapter 2
Ancient worlds

Greece and Rome

Homer's *Iliad* and *Odyssey*, which had long existed in the oral tradition, were written down on parchment or papyrus sheet in the 8th century BCE. These were copied over the centuries until, after Gutenberg's invention of the printing press, they finally reached the safety of print. In the ancient world, and for hundreds of years after, for the vast majority, these texts were listened to. A great deal is known about reading in the ancient Greek and Roman worlds but it is important to remember that a good deal of what we think of as Greek and Roman literature was heard and not read. The Greek and Roman Empires included readers, but it was orality—and the expert use of rhetoric—that remained the prized preserves of intellectuals. In fact writing and reading were often seen as both socially and politically disruptive, and an intellectual cheat.

Plato, for example, expressed reservations in his *Phaedrus*, a dialogue between Socrates and Phaedrus, and he has the latter declare, 'Every word, when once it is written, is bandied about, alike among those who understand it and those who have no interest in it, and it knows not to whom to speak or not to speak…When ill-treated or unjustly abused it [the word] always needs its father to help it; for it has no power to protect or help

itself.' For Plato, like many ancients, 'spoken discourse' was
the language of truth and written discourse always subject to
'misreading' or 'misinterpretation'. Reading aloud was one thing as
there could be discussion and debate about what the text meant.
During his lifetime, language and its practice had developed to a
point where abstract concepts could be extensively investigated.
This idea of a text becoming part of the reader was viewed with
some suspicion, and it was these extraordinary changes in reading
practice that Plato wrote into his famous dialogue, known as
Phaedrus. The exchange between Socrates and Phaedrus is mostly
about the nature of love, but it also explores writing and reading.
Socrates tells Phaedrus that long ago the god Troth visited the
King of Egypt and offered him some of the disciplines he'd
invented including writing. 'Here', said Troth, 'is a branch of
learning that will improve their [the King's subjects] memories;
my discovery provides a recipe for both memory and wisdom.'
The King was doubtful: 'If men learn this', he told Troth,

> their souls will be implanted with forgetfulness; they will cease to
> exercise memory because they will rely on that which is written,
> calling things to remembrance from no longer within themselves,
> but by means of external marks. What you have discovered is not a
> recipe for memory but for reminder. And it is no true wisdom that
> you offer your disciples, but only its semblance, for by telling them
> of many things without teaching them anything, you will make
> them seem to know much, while for the most part they will know
> nothing. And as men not filled with wisdom but conceit of wisdom,
> they will be a burden to their fellow-men.

Socrates continues:

> You know, Phaedrus, that's the strange thing about writing, which
> makes it truly analogous to painting. The painter's products stand
> before us as though they were alive: but if you question them,
> they maintain a most majestic silence. It is the same with written

words: they seem to talk to you as though they were intelligent, but if you question them about what they say, from a desire to be instructed, they go on telling you just the same thing for ever.

This is a key debate about writing—and reading. The creative role of the reader was something that had barely existed in oral society when meaning was understood more or less immediately. Plato, who was both Socrates' pupil and biographer, seems, on first sight, to have sought to uphold his master's position. But he did so *in writing*, suggesting, perhaps, that he advocated the 'proper' use of writing, or the use of writing by only a select group. Plato banished poets from his ideal society, outlined in his *Republic*, however. Knowledge—in the mouths and hands of the right people—could be a resource to further the common good. Poetry and fiction, on the other hand, were clearly to be feared.

Slowly but surely, however, reading aloud in a group gave way to solitary, silent reading. And when we think of reading we think primarily of this secret, silent act, carried out alone. By the 5th century BCE reading was becoming a skill used for accessing information. Thucydides (c.460–395 BCE), a historian and politician, was writing accounts of the past that depended more on the written word than the oral. This is evidence of a telling shift in the way the written word was understood. Rather than acting as a script for oral performance, the written word had come to be seen as a repository of knowledge, one whose contents transcended time.

Physicians like Hippocrates (c.460–377 BCE) and Galen (c. AD 130–200) extended and spread knowledge in a way that had been impossible in a wholly oral society. Of Hippocrates, Galen wrote, 'I shall interpret those observations [of Hippocrates] which are too obscure, and add others of my own, arrived at by the methods he wrote down.' Reading allowed for a much more deliberate and critical assimilation of others' thoughts on which the writer could then base and extend ideas, theories, and arguments across time.

More extensive use of reading encouraged other kinds of writing, in particular the ancient novel, a new literary genre, and one which would gradually become the dominant literary genre globally. These were stories of love, loss, and reunion, usually involving a man and woman of high birth. There were also heroic tales of bravery and superhuman endeavour. These stories remained widely read until about the 6th century when they seem to have lost popularity. By the 11th century their appeal re-established itself and influenced the Arabic, then Spanish, and then pan-European novel-reading and writing scene.

Silent reading

The subject of silent reading has aroused a good deal of debate. A famous passage in St Augustine's *Confessions* (4th century CE) accounts for many of the misunderstandings. He described his teacher's practice of silent reading. Of St Ambrose, Bishop of Milan, Augustine wrote:

> When he was reading, he drew his eyes along over the leaves, and his heart searched into its sense, but his voice and tongue were silent. Oft-times when we were present…we still saw him reading to himself, and never otherwise.…But with what intent soever he did it, that man certainly had a good meaning to it.

Now Augustine's surprise at Ambrose's reading method was interpreted as evidence that silent reading was very rare at the time and that the common practice must have been reading aloud. This presumption was widely shared. Nietzsche, for example, wrote: 'The German does not read aloud, does not read for the ear but merely with his eyes: he has put his ears in the drawer. In antiquity, when a man read—which he did very seldom—he read to himself…in a loud voice; it was a matter of surprise if someone read quietly, and people secretly asked themselves why he did so. In a loud voice: that is to say, with all the crescendos, inflections, variations of tone, and changes of tempo in which the ancient public world took pleasure.' What Nietzsche goes on to argue is that the greatest German prose was written for the pulpit. The greatest work, he claims, is Luther's Bible, intended to be read out in churches.

But there is evidence that some private, silent reading went on in the classical period. For example, Euripides (c.480–406 BCE) in his tragedy *Hippolytus* has Theseus, the king, confronted by the corpse of his wife, Phaedra, and finds a letter fastened to her hand. While the Chorus expresses its foreboding, Theseus reads the letter—silently. In the letter, Phaedra falsely accuses Hippolytus of having raped her. His silent reading then contrasts with his emotional remonstrations. The letter, he says, 'shrieks, it howls horrors insufferable…a voice from the letter speaks…'. Plutarch (c.46–120 CE), in a speech entitled 'On the Fortune of Alexander', tells us that when Alexander the Great was reading a confidential letter from his mother—silently—his friend Hephaestion 'quietly put his head beside Alexander's and read the letter with him; Alexander could not bear to stop him, but took off his ring and placed the seal on Hephaestion's lips.' The story is told four times, presumably for emphasis. Alexander doesn't become angry with his friend's presumptuous reading over his shoulder, but behaves like a philosopher, indicating to his friend, in a discreet way, that the correspondence is highly confidential.

In order to read aloud effectively, particularly before words were separated by spacing—they were run together in the classical world—you need to be able to look ahead of what you are enunciating, as musicians must when reading music. Silent reading, arguably, is a necessary adjunct to reading aloud for sound but also, crucially, for sense. What shocked Augustine, some classicists have argued, was that Ambrose read silently in company. He was reading in front of visitors but didn't share his reading with them. This may have been unusual, even, perhaps, deemed impolite. But Gavrilov, one of the great authorities in the matter of silent reading, concludes that the phenomenon of reading is essentially the same in modern culture as it was in the ancient world. Cultural diversity does not mean that there cannot be an underlying unity.

Sappho

Although the practice of reading may have changed relatively little across time, what we make of our reading certainly has. Take the case of Sappho *c.*630—*c.*570 BCE.

Sappho is undoubtedly the most famous and intriguing ancient Greek woman reader. Her contemporaries praised her in hyperbolic fashion and some regarded her as the tenth Muse. She continued to be widely read until the Middle Ages. Strabo, the Greek stoic scholar (*c.*63/4 BCE–*c.*24 CE), wrote of her several hundred years after her death, 'in this whole span of recorded time we know of no woman to challenge her as a poet even in the slightest degree'. Christine de Pizan lists Sappho in her *Cité des dames* (1405; translated as 'The Book of the City of Ladies'), as one of the eighteen proofs that women are as intellectually able as men. In the early Renaissance, Raphael includes Sappho in his painting of the wise on Mount Parnassus. She is the only mortal to have been included. Skipping forward again, we find Victorian women naming Sappho most frequently in a poll (*The Pall Mall Gazette*) asking readers to name the twelve most important women in history. Only tantalizing fragments of her nine books survive, and quotations and references to her in ancient authors, and scraps of ancient papyrus and parchment copies, mostly from the Roman period. These texts number 264 in modern editions but only sixty-three contain complete lines and only twenty-one contain complete verses. Only four poems have survived in sufficient wholeness for us to have a proper sense of Sapphic poetic structure.

Nevertheless what little we have of Sappho is strikingly different from what remains of her male contemporaries, like Hesiod and

Alcaeus, most particularly. Sappho's distinctively feminine voice comes through. There is an emotional range, reservations about war and violence, a striking sense of individuality, and a portrayal of women that is quite different from other contemporary representations. Take fragment 16:

> Some say an army of horsemen, some an army on foot and some
> say a fleet of ships is the loveliest sight ... but I say it is what-ever
> you desire ...

Helen of Troy is described by Sappho as desiring a man who was not her husband, and her passion is presented as more rational than that of men's want of fleets of ships. Alcaeus, on the other hand, wrote bluntly of Helen: 'But through Helen, the Trojans perished | and all their city.' Sappho introduced a new range of human feeling into Greek poetry and for this she was highly respected. But her image today is based on a limited number of fragments which can be reconstructed to exaggerate—or dramatically downplay—her importance.

Sappho intrigues us in part because she is such an early poetess. But she also fascinates us because unlike many of her male contemporaries, Homer most obviously, whose works remain as good as intact, Sappho is something of a clean slate onto which others can—and have—projected myriad fantasies. And the echoes of Sappho in poets from Ovid to T. S. Eliot create an extraordinarily rich afterlife for her across the millennia. Catullus imitated her—a sure sign of respect. Much later, however, there were noteworthy detractors. Alexander Pope described a woman author of his period (Lady Mary Wortley Montagu) not only as a 'promiscuous Sappho' but a syphilitic one into the bargain. By the 19th century women were boldly reading Sappho for feminist inspiration. The Victorian poet Christina Rossetti, for example, explicitly described her as a role model. During the same period men read Sappho rather differently. Baudelaire and Swinburne saw her as a sado-masochistic and androgynous *femme fatale*.

Reading Sappho has clearly often been more a matter of reinvention of her words in the mind of the reader. Indeed she has been so reinvented that her unique voice has almost been silenced—in other readers' subsequent revoicing of her. This is perhaps still more obvious in visual representations of her, like so many other accomplished women, who have been the subject of a male voyeuristic gaze. Yet we need to remember, once again, that we have so very little of Sappho actually to read. And we are also reminded that much of reading is about inventing our own fantasies on the basis of what we read.

Reading material in the Roman Empire

The concept of empire was the first impetus towards a society in which literacy was more widespread. Of all ancient societies it was Roman society that promoted reading and writing among more than a small bureaucratic and priestly elite. The requirements of complex legal and military systems to govern a vast empire stretching across most of what is now Western Europe (from Britain to North Africa and from Spain to the Danube in today's Germany) were predicated on accurate written communication.

Writing was everywhere to be seen in public urban areas—on monuments, on outdoor altars, on sarcophagi, on boundary markers, and so on. At the height of empire (*c.*117 BCE), soldiers and craftspeople were literate, at least to a rudimentary degree. Graffiti found at various sites, at Herculaneum, Ostia, and Pompeii, for example, testify to this. Some of the graffiti at Pompeii may be the work of prostitutes warning their colleagues of the danger posed by certain clients. But despite growing literacy and the recognition of its many merits, orality remained the medium of literary culture. The wealthy expected to be read to, and readers were employed, or slaves kept, precisely for the purpose. Pliny the Younger (*c.* AD 62–*c.*113), writer, administrator, and prolific letter-writer, frequently recorded his pleasure in being read to:

> At dinner, when my wife is present or a few friends, I have a book read aloud; after dinner a comedy or lyre playing; afterwards a stroll with my people, among whom are erudite individuals. Thus the evening passes in varied discussions, and even the longest day is quickly seasoned.

For the Emperor Augustus (63 BCE–14 CE), listening to reading countered insomnia. His biographer, Suetonius (*c.*75–150 CE), records how he would summon story-tellers to his bedside. Reading aloud would mostly be from scrolls and in the first centuries epic poems constituted the most popular genre. Authors also read their works. Virgil (70–19 BCE) was celebrated for his performances which allowed the illiterate to hear his works. Ovid (43 BCE–17/18 CE) wrote for a wide audience and in a number of genres. His *Ars amatoria* (*The Art of Love*) and *Remedia amoris* (*Love's Remedy*) are essentially self-help books for women, advice about how to attract love, advising the reading of poetry among other things, and a consoling work for those who have been unlucky in love, respectively.

Ovid was writing at a time when a large number of new types of popular texts appeared including erotica, potted histories, cookery books, books of popular psychology, including interpretations of dreams, for example, and adventure stories. Something akin to gossip columns were written into contemporary satires. Readers' enjoyment of scandal and instinct to scapegoat are by no means the result of digital social media. Martial (40–*c.*103 CE) wrote twelve books of *Epigrams* in which he makes fun of the activities of his urban acquaintances, including women and homosexuals. But the growing enfranchisement of less-educated audiences had its critics. The philosopher Seneca (3 BCE–65 CE) famously deplored those who used books as no more than interior decoration. He despised owners of scrolls with decorated knobs and coloured labels designed primarily for display.

Scholarly libraries were also a feature of Roman culture. Some of the holdings were the spoils of war: the library of the Macedonian king Perseus was brought to Rome in the 2nd century BCE by Aemilius Paulus, and the library of Apellicon of Teos, which included many of Aristotle's books, was looted by Sulla from Athens. Julius Caesar, perhaps surprisingly, did not found a library in Rome. The first public library was the work of G. Asinius Pollio. Augustus founded two more: in the Temple of Apollo on the Palatine hill, and in the Portico of Octavia at the Campus Martius. Public libraries were often housed in the same buildings as public baths. At its highpoint there were twenty-nine libraries in Rome. There were also libraries in the provinces. Pliny the younger paid for the library in his native Como in Northern Italy. Libraries were also founded at Ephesus (now in modern Turkey), and in Athens. Some libraries allowed book borrowing in certain circumstances. For reasons that haven't altogether been explained, there were only two libraries in the empire west of Italy: in Carthage (Tunisia) and in Timgad (Algeria).

Chapter 3
Reading manuscripts, reading print

Reading manuscripts

The codex had been adopted as the standard format for writing in the late Roman Empire; it remained the normal format throughout the so-called Middle Ages in Western Europe until the invention of print in the middle of the 15th century. For some the whole Western—at least—intellectual tradition has been shaped almost exclusively by the invention of print. For roughly a millennium, from 500 to 1500, manuscript culture was the culture of writing and reading. The medium was parchment, the readers were mostly clerics and aristocrats, and the language was Latin. The practice of illumination continued and the form of the book, the codex, lasted too.

Throughout medieval Europe, reading was intimately bound up with religion, specifically with Christianity, which, like Judaism and Islam, is essentially a religion of the book. But this was not wholly a new beginning. Respect, even nostalgia, for the classical learning of Greece and Rome remained, sometimes in conflict with the ideas and beliefs of the ever-expanding Christian Church. By the late 6th century the papacy was entrenched and powerful enough to establish a new Christian form of Roman imperialism and Christian books travelled in large numbers across Western Europe. In 587, for example, Gregory the Great sent 'all the books that would be necessary', according to Bede, the 8th-century Benedictine monk and chronicler, for the conversion of the English. During the 7th and 8th centuries Irish strands of Christianity were assimilated in Britain and books combining the English and Irish styles were produced, like the Vespasian Psalter, most likely penned in Canterbury, which includes detailed pictures inside letters, very much in the Irish tradition.

In the late 8th century Charlemagne took control of the now-established Franco-German territories. Alcuin (c.742–814) was summoned from England to found a sumptuous and extensive palace library. At the same time scripts were standardized into an easily legible round style. Centres of book production sprang up in monasteries all over Western Europe, sometimes producing codices for their own use, sometimes for export. Charlemagne's *Admonitio Generalis* (789), a work designed to maintain Christian control, emphasized the need for improvements, specifically in literacy and education more broadly. This advice was aimed at priests to facilitate the consolidation of the Frankish Church. Most priests, at this point, were illiterate and peripatetic, and relied solely on what they assimilated aurally from the teachers of Scripture and the Church Fathers. Meanwhile it was Carolingian scribes who copied every extant work of literature. A fragment of the catalogue of the Aachen library lists a large number of classical works. Charlemagne is responsible not only for founding the modern Christian Church, but also for preserving Western written culture much more broadly.

Although there were exceptions, medieval reading was almost always a group activity. And it was an activity that took place in a variety of different places: gardens and halls, marketplaces, churches, and monasteries. Readers were no longer paid servants or slaves, but members of the family, friends, or associates. Reading, as in the ancient world, largely remained being read *to*. Literacy rates remained low, perhaps 1 per cent of the population, books were expensive, and few people ever spent leisure time alone. The shift from a largely oral culture to a literate culture was a slow one, beginning with the wealthiest and most powerful, the aristocracy and clergy, and slowly filtering its way down to the poorest and least privileged, some 1,200 years later. It is a shift marked by three essential changes: what is written invites interpretation, a decoding that goes beyond what is possible with oral engagement; 'history' can be conceived of in a wholly new way as texts can be assembled and compared; and the written text becomes an object, one which is often seen as of great aesthetic beauty—and value.

Solitary, silent reading generally became more and more the norm, with the reader participating in a private and secret engagement. The reader can establish his or her own tempo, can look back in order to reread, can take a break from reading to reflect, and can even make marginal notes. The possibility of considering different *interpretations* of a text is also greatly facilitated. With silent reading comes a new sense of the self as a thinking individual, free to agree or disagree with what is read. And all this mostly without censorship or possible punishment. Silent reading became common throughout Europe during the 13th century. It also became scholars' preferred and championed method of reading. A Cistercian prior in south-west Germany in the 13th century, one Richalm von Schöntal, told a story in which demons had forced him to read aloud. This, he claimed, had robbed him of proper spiritual insight and spiritual sustenance. He, like other Cistercian monks of the time, regarded the heart as the locus of the mind.

From the 12th century on, increasing numbers of lay people became book owners and commissioners of books. A significant change in the landscape of literacy was the increasing number of women readers. They might own their own prayer books, in the form of books of hours, which allowed them both to perfect their own reading skills and also to provide their children with the basics of literacy. Women—who rarely received a classical education—were also highly influential in the move to produce books in the vernacular languages of every day, particularly French and German, rather than Latin. Remarkably, by the 14th century, the volume of manuscript production in the vernaculars was competing with the volume of works produced by the clergy in Latin. This is important to underline as it is a reminder that the world of reading had changed dramatically *before* the invention of the printing press. The book culture was a precursor, not the product, of printing. All the necessary features of a book culture existed before the invention of the printing press: readers, both clerical and lay, men and women, reading in both Latin and, increasingly, the vernaculars.

One of the most read types of books among the laity was the book of hours. These were made up of various prayers appropriate for different times of day and different points in the liturgical year. Patrons might commission a personalized book to suit their own devotional practices. Some were lavishly and richly illuminated. They were mostly produced in Latin, in Gothic script, from the 12th century on, and thus accessible to lay readers, including educated women aristocrats, who were often the owners of these beautiful, portable objects. An outstanding example is *Les Très Riches Heures du Duc de Berry*, produced for the Duke (1340–1416) who was the brother of Charles V of France.

He was a book-collector and generous patron of the arts. His book of hours took years to complete and in fact the duke died before it was finished. Like many of the most sumptuous books of hours it was produced by groups of artists. It was begun by the Flemish Limbourg brothers and was then worked on by the Flemish craftsman Barthélemy d'Eyck (*c.*1420–post-1470). It was completed under the patronage of Charles, Duke of Savoy (1468–90), around 1485. In all John, Duke of Berry commissioned more than a dozen books of hours and at the time of his death his library contained more than 300 illuminated manuscripts.

The rise of silent reading more or less coincided with the rise in reading material enjoyed outside the authority of the Church. Large amounts of material that had circulated only in oral form were committed to paper: ancient myths, tales, and legends, the Arthurian legends in particular, were all written down. But they still functioned as scripts to be read aloud. In France, these were the writings of the troubadours, *The Poem of the Cid*, *The Song of Roland*, and, in the late 12th century, the romances of Chrétien de Troyes. Chrétien declared, poetically, that the classical literature of the Greeks and Romans had been superseded: 'There is no more word of them; their glowing embers are extinguished.' And in the 1300s, Durante degli Alighieri, commonly known as Dante, the Italian poet of the Late Middle Ages, defending Italian over Latin in Italy in the 1300s, claimed that Italian had come of age as the language of literature.

Reading in your own language

Lay audiences in the High Middle Ages were reading not simply material from the oral tradition that had been written down, but new stories too, in various vernaculars including Old French, Middle High German, Middle English, Old Spanish, Old Norse, and numerous others. Remarkably the manner in which people read was changing fundamentally also. Works in the vernacular languages could be small and modest in appearance, or lavishly illustrated and illuminated. One of the most illustrious patrons of writings in the vernacular was Alfonso X of Castile (1221–84). His interests were wide-ranging. He commissioned a remarkable series of songs (*Cantigas*) in praise of the Virgin Mary. Each page is made up of six miniatures; these are highly detailed illuminated illustrations with captions. Alfonso was also interested in law and commissioned a multi-volume set of treatises, *Libra de las leyes* ('Book of the Laws'), and a series of chronicles, making up a history of Spain, and written in Castilian.

Book patronage could be nothing more than an outward sign of wealth and power but in most cases patrons were committed to the book as a cultural artefact and cultural force. If what a wealthy individual believed should be available to be read, or wanted to read, was unavailable, then that book could be commissioned—or written. Julian of Norwich, one of the great English mystics, was a great reader and harvester of what she read, and may have written one of the first books in English by a woman, *Sixteen Revelations of Divine Love* (*c*.1393).

Among these promoters of book culture and reading were a surprising number of remarkable women. Christine de Pizan (*c*.1364–1430) was born in Venice and well educated. She married young and was widowed. After her husband's death she turned to writing. What is particularly interesting about this particular woman author is that her writings are so clearly a response to her reading. It was her reading of Matheolus' *Lamenta* (1300), a virulent attack on women, that prompted her to write *Le Livre de la cité des dames* (*The Book of the City of Ladies*), which she completed in 1405 (see Figure 6).

She begins with a reflection on men's attitudes to women, expressed in speech, and writing:

> An extraordinary thought became planted in my mind which made me wonder why on earth it is that so many men...have said and continue to say and write such awful things about women and their ways. I was at a loss as to how to explain it. It is not just a handful of writers who do this...It is all manner of philosophers, orators and poets too numerous to mention, who all seem to speak with one voice and are unanimous in their view that female nature is wholly given up to vice.

The utopian women's city envisaged by Christine is refined not as a function of birth, but as a function of their reading. In *La Cité* arguments for the education of women are proposed and questions

6. **Christine de Pizan,** *Le Livre de la cité des dames.*

are asked about men's reluctance to see women educated. According to Christine, women are innately suited to reading and study.

Print

Until the middle of the 15th century reading involved an intimate encounter between a reader and a scribe. What was read was a unique hand-produced or hand-copied manuscript. Then, round about 1440, a young engraver and gemstone carver had an ingenious idea. Instead of carving wooden blocks to reproduce illustrations—which was already in practice—why not cut letters out to produce reusable 'type'? Over a period of some years, he invested very large sums of money in his risky entrepreneurial venture which involved adapting mechanical instruments used in wine-making and book-binding. The craftsman who came up with this ingenious idea was, of course, Johannes Gensleisch zur Laden zum Gutenberg, known to us as Johann Gutenberg, or even just Gutenberg. He was not solely responsible for its invention in the 1440s, he was one of a team, working in Mainz. The arrival of the printed book, like most dramatic innovations, was regarded by some as a temporary fad. Johannes Trithemius, an abbot at Sponheim, wrote in *In Praise of Scribes* in 1492, almost half a century after the invention of the printing press: 'How long will printing something on paper last?...At the most a paper book could last two hundred years...Writing on parchment...can last for a thousand years.' The best parchment, calfskin (vellum) had indeed been the chosen support for the finest manuscript production for centuries.

The invention of the printing press was in many ways a revolutionary innovation. But the origins and consequences of its invention are numerous and sometimes contradictory. And its consequences for reading are still more difficult to assess. Nor indeed was this a wholly novel invention. Movable metal type had been used to print in Korea in the 13th century, although without a press. Printed books did not, however, immediately become affordable. The printing mechanism was relatively inexpensive to build, but the cost of paper remained high until the 18th century. Until this time the cost of paper accounted for more than half the total cost of a book. This meant that increasing the size of print runs did not reduce an individual book's retail price, as is the case today. Paper making was still based on the Arabic method which involved pulping rags and unwanted cloth collected by 'ragpickers' throughout Europe.

Between 1450 and 1455 Gutenberg printed a bible—the first ever book printed from movable type. And presses were soon established throughout Europe: in Italy in 1465, in France in 1470, in Spain in 1472, in Holland and England in 1475. By the 1480s there were presses in urban centres in Germany, Italy, the Netherlands, England, and Denmark. By the 16th century there were also presses in Switzerland, Scandinavia, and Eastern Europe. Spanish and Portuguese missionaries introduced printing to South America and Japan. Interestingly, the printing press didn't reach the New World until 1533 when a press was set up in Mexico City. And it wasn't until 1638 that Cambridge, Massachusetts, had a printing press.

But while historians make a convincing case, economists, until recently, have been unable to prove that the printing press—and the increase in reading that came with it—made any difference to productivity and the economy in increasingly literate societies. Some economists have even concluded that the economic impact of the printing press was limited and this would mean, by extension, that reading and literacy were equally marginal to the economies of the 16th century. But a recent study examined data on cities in relation to the diffusion and adoption of the printing press and examined the technology's impact from a new perspective. This showed that after the adoption of the printing press cities grew by at least 20 percentage points, and in some cases as much as 78 percentage points, more than similar cities that did not adopt printing in the period 1500–1600. These estimates suggest that the impact of the printing press accounted for at least 18 per cent and as much as 68 per cent of European city growth between 1500 and 1600. It is likely that reading was key to economic growth in the period.

In a woodcut from 1568 (see Figure 7), the printer on the left is removing a newly printed page from the press, while the one on the right is inking the text-blocks for the next impression. From old price tables it has been calculated that, around 1600, a printing press could produce some 3,500 impressions per day. This is based on what we know of the average day's work for workmen around the time—a gruelling fifteen hours. The movable-type printing press was clearly the great innovation in early modern information technology. But what difference did the advent of the printing press make to people's lives? For the first time in human history it was possible to reproduce reading material quickly and in very large quantities. And, of course,

7. Woodcut, printing in the 16th century.

printed books were very much cheaper than manuscripts. Within fifty years of its invention, the price of books dropped by roughly 66 per cent. This made a dramatic difference to the way ideas spread, speeding up the process and widening the domains in which they circulated.

The Reformation and the rise of literacy

Gutenberg's invention coincided with, and of course further fuelled, another profoundly significant event, a major theological schism in Western Christianity—the Protestant Reformation. In 1519 the Roman theologian Sylvester Prierias declared that the Bible had to remain a 'mystery' and that it could only be truthfully transmitted through the power and authority of the Pope. Luther, by contrast, claimed that God's grace descended as a function of individual faith and not through the agency of the Church and he, and others of like mind, particularly in Germany, the Netherlands, and Switzerland, argued that everyone—man, woman, and child—had the 'divine right' to read. Luther's position wasn't altogether new but the circumstances were.

The invention of printing, together with the German princes' desire to break free from the controlling power of Rome, conspired to protect Luther and to allow for the dissemination of his ideas. Luther protested against indulgences, for example, and this led to the production of literally thousands of poorly written and cheaply produced pamphlets that circulated throughout the Holy Roman Empire. So this is a moment of extraordinary historical coincidence. Printing promoted the Reformation and the Protestant reformers promoted literacy and reading, which in turn supported the rise of print culture. Bibles were translated into the vernaculars—that's to say the languages of everyday life—which meant that everyone who could read, could read the Bible, regardless of whether or not they had had a classical education. Erasmus, who kept his distance from Luther and looked for reform within the Church, nevertheless shared Luther's conviction that direct access to the Bible was in the interests of the faith. Erasmus wrote, 'I wish that even the weakest woman should read the Gospel—should read the Epistles of St Paul. And I wish that these were translated into all the languages so that they might be read and understood, not only by Scots and Irishmen, but also by Turks and Saracens' (by which he meant Muslims). When Luther was working on his German translation of the Bible he advised those who were helping him, 'You must ask the woman in her house, the children in the streets, the common man in the market, and look at their mouths, how they speak and translate that way; then they'll understand and see that you're speaking to them in German.'

The Protestant Reformation, the Renaissance, and the scientific revolution of the 17th century are all dependent on a sophisticated network of print cultures. Print changed not just the way we read, but the way we think. But, surprisingly, manuscript culture survived for some time after the advent of printing. The circulation of manuscript books, particularly in England and Spain, continued unabated, particularly works of poetry and romances. Writers continued to write specifically for scribal transmission.

The first printers worked for specific groups: the wealthy, churchmen, lawyers, and scholars. Printers were quick to see the market for new types of textual production including almanacs, for example, often produced in very large numbers and sold to the general public. But print-runs were relatively small, with the exception of almanacs, and prayer books. These were printed in runs of tens of thousands and sold in both urban and rural areas by itinerant vendors. It wasn't until the 19th century that most printing runs exceeded 1,000, occasionally 1,500 copies. The reading of prayers was often more than a matter of inner spiritual nourishment. For example, by the early 16th century, the prayer beginning *Deus propicius esto michi* ('God have mercy upon me') was deemed to bring about a variety of effects: calming storms at sea, protecting the soldier in battle and the new-born baby on delivery, and so on. In the 16th century, in England at the court of Edward VI, women used to wear often beautifully decorated books tied to their belts. This may have been motivated by superstition, a belief in the book's protective powers.

How did reading change with the advent of print? It's an intriguing question to which we only have some answers. People's familiarity with the written word, and perhaps pleasure in it, weren't immediately displaced by the book. And Gutenberg and other early printers sought to imitate handwriting in print. The vast majority of *incunabula*, as books are generally known pre-1501, look very much like manuscripts. In fact the art of handwriting, paradoxically, was promoted by printing. Large numbers of manuals were published demonstrating the art of beautiful handwriting. Books, like manuscripts, continued to be objects of great value, both pecuniary and aesthetic. Books were sold unbound, in gathered sheets, and, depending on the new owner, bound at greater or lesser expense. Large bound volumes of the Bible, for example, measuring 30 cm by 40 cm, if bound in vellum, would have required the skins of some 200 sheep. Soon publishers produced smaller and more manageable editions and books became less objects of conspicuous wealth but rather objects of intellectual aspiration or attainment. By the end of the 16th century readers' demands had begun to change. Affordability became the primary requirement for the majority of book-buyers. Printers responded by publishing cheaper books. Their most important market was no longer men and women of letters, but a much broader readership. Money was to be made simply producing cheap editions of the Church Fathers, other popular religious works, and reprints of best-selling titles that had proved their popularity.

Individual readers

By the second quarter of the 16th century only one copy of *The Book of Margery Kempe* existed. The work is a record of the experiences and mystical visions of Margery (*c*.1373–*c*.1439), who left her husband in order to devote her life to religion. She travelled widely, to Jerusalem, Rome, Compostela, and Bad Wilsnack, in the German state of Brandenburg. Until 1539 the book was in the Carthusian charterhouse's library of Mount Grace Priory in Yorkshire, England. It was heavily annotated by between four and six readers. One monk who has become known as the Red Ink Annotator has left fascinating traces of his reading both in the margins and interlinearly. No modern reader of the manuscript can fail to be influenced by his interpretations and recastings of Margery's accounts of her life and more specifically of the temptations of the flesh she experienced and her trial for heresy. The Red Ink Annotator emerges as a reader intent on glossing Margery so as to cast her as a model of devotion for lay women readers as well as a perfect object of contemplation for Carthusians. His annotations ensure that Margery cannot be read as having erred in terms of either her physical life or her spiritual and intellectual life, flirting, for example, with the unorthodox. Margery's writings are an early reminder that what we read is never unadulterated. What we read is never previously unread when it comes to us. And reading a modern edition of Margery's *Book*, without the markings of the Red Ink Annotator, we cannot know in what ways it may have been altered since it left the protection of its author.

As was feared by those who opposed the changes brought by the Reformation some individuals read naively or 'misread'. One remarkable example was a miller, Domenico Scandella (1532–99), also known as Menocchio, from the Friuli in modern northern Italy. He read both the Bible and a number of other works in the vernacular and conceived of his own cosmology of the world, believing, for example, that the world was made out of excrement. He was tried for heresy and the documents that were produced during his trial provide an extraordinary insight not only into what this 16th-century miller read, but *how* he read, mistaking, for example, the metaphorical for the literal. And this kind of independent reading and thinking cost him his life and he was burnt at the stake.

Individual readers went about reading in ways which were conditioned by gender, class, and race, no doubt. But there are myriad other variables ranging from the specificities of circumstance, place, religious affiliations, social circle, the nature of the individual's education, etc. There is some fascinating evidence of individual readers worth considering. John Dawson (1692–1765), who worked for the London tax office, bequeathed his library to his local parish church and it has survived. He owned over 100 books and kept them carefully catalogued. This was not unusual for a man of his class. He was especially interested in history. But what is of more particular interest is evidence of the way in which he *used* his books: to some degree they formed the basis of an elaborate filing system that allowed him to create his own annotated and supplemented books. First, he would correct printing errors and add any missing basic material, including page numbers, for example. He also wrote notes in the margins which give us some insight into what drew his attention as he read. He would compose chronologies, lists of historical figures, and indexes which allowed him to find the interleaved pages of his own handwritten addenda. Dawson's *use* of books went beyond reading, much like the use of manuscripts in the pre-print era. Research in the British Library's rare books collection has established that Dawson's use of books was common at the time. Other books show similar signs that they have been used as a starting point for the elaboration of a personalized version of the books being read. Addenda entitled 'The Signification of the Marks in this Book', keys to marginal annotations, for example, suggest that readers expected to return to the book after some considerable interval, hence needing an aide-memoire to explain the shorthand.

There is no evidence to suggest that all early modern readers used books in this way but the existence of large numbers of manuscript books does substantiate the idea that most readers read pen in hand, copying out sections that were of particular interest to them. Reading was, in a sense, a matter of taking the essentials from a book and noting them down for future reference. The existence of commonplace books is further evidence of how people read during this period. The format was a printed book with headings which also appeared in an index. The idea was that while reading, the reader could copy notes into the commonplace book, under the appropriate heading, allowing for the easy retrieval of reading nuggets at a later stage. It is a format that beautifully marries reading and writing and was undoubtedly the most important intellectual tool for classifying knowledge in the early modern period. It is a model of reading first proposed by the great humanist Erasmus in his *De utraque verborum ac rerum copia* ('Copia: Foundations of the Abundant Style'), also known as *De copia verborum* (1513).

From the 15th century on most church traditions encouraged literacy for both boys and girls, and parents were encouraged to provide their children and other members of their household with a Christian education. The practice of learning the Ten Commandments, of reciting psalms and prayers, and becoming familiar with Bible readings, all encouraged broader reading skills. But despite the teaching of these basic reading skills, few ordinary people became prolific readers, in part because of a lack of reading material. It remained the case, from the 15th century until the 18th, that the vast majority of serious readers—as we might call them—were members of the aristocracy, the clergy and women religious, doctors, and wealthy merchants. Some less wealthy tradesmen—and indeed tradeswomen—exercised their literacy skills in their work but few owned books. And the limited number of books owned by the literate went hand in hand with 'intensive reading' as it has become known in the history of the book. All but the wealthy, who might collect and have established their own private libraries, or those who had access to medieval university libraries, for example, would read and reread a limited number of books. But a literate 'middle class', we might say, slowly emerged. Crudely speaking the end of the Middle Ages marked the beginning of a gradual rise of a middle class that began to control new economic and commercial enterprises. With wealth came an increased desire to play a part in political processes (further fuelled by and fuelling the rise of newspapers) and a wish to participate in cultural activities which had previously been the almost exclusive privilege of the wealthy.

Chapter 4
Modern reading

The Industrial Revolution, from the late 18th century on, brought changes to reading. Printing processes developed further, in particular typesetting. Friedrich Koenig (1774–1833) developed a printing press powered by steam. The first commercial unit was bought by the *Times* of London in 1814. It could print 1,100 copies per hour, which was a very significant improvement on hand-operated presses. And it was principally Koenig's steam-machine, combined with cheaper paper-making, that accounts for the birth, and rapid rise, of the 'daily'.

Newspapers were widely circulated and widely read. Then, in 1835, the first commercial 'web' press was invented. Instead of printing a whole series of sheets of paper, a 'web', or continuous roll of paper was used. The paper was then cut into 'pages' after it had been printed. Finally, in 1844, Richard Hoe (1812–86) in the United States developed the rotary press (see Figure 8). This press could print an astonishing 20,000 copies per hour. Meanwhile, the coming of the railways in many parts of the world allowed for the much faster transportation of printed goods. People moved too—and in very large numbers.

The Industrial Revolution (including printing and its knock-on effects), which developed quickly in England 1750–1850, and spread to the Continent after the Napoleonic Wars, brought about

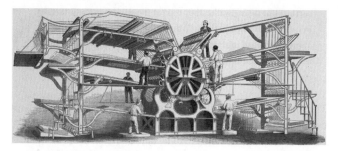

8. Richard Hoe's rotary press.

other profound changes including the expansion of towns and
cities. Throughout Europe, only 17 per cent of the population lived
in cities in 1801 but by 1851, only fifty years later, the percentage
had increased to 35 per cent, and by 1891, it was 54 per cent. The
growth of cities was most marked in England in the first half of
the 19th century with an 'industrial Midlands'—Manchester,
Birmingham, and Leeds—developing in an area which, only some
half-century earlier, had been almost completely rural. Meanwhile
the great capitals and cities of London, Paris, Vienna, Berlin,
Rome, Madrid, and New York grew apace.

Towns and cities inevitably became the privileged places for
reading. Books found their way into rural areas, of course, but the
immediate availability of reading material in urban areas gave them
a distinct edge particularly given that literacy rates also tended to be
higher in the towns and cities, and leisure time, while limited for
the majority, was greater than in rural areas. Faster means of
transport and associated modern postal services improved matters.
It is perhaps only the internet that has really levelled the playing
field in terms of urban and rural readers on material available in
that medium. One German tourist, at the end of the 18th century,
penned an astonished account of the state of affairs in Paris:

> Everyone is reading…Everyone, but women in particular, is
> carrying a book around in their pocket. People read while riding in

carriages or taking walks; they read at the theatre in the interval, in cafés, even when bathing. Women, children, journeymen and apprentices read in shops. On Sundays people read while seated at the front of their houses; lackeys read on their back seats, coachmen up on their boxes, and soldiers keeping guard.

The model for free, compulsory education was Prussian, established in 1717 by Frederick William I, and further developed by his son Frederick II in 1763. The approach was adopted in the Austrian Empire in 1774. By the 18th century, in England, a fortuitous combination of events conspired further to boost reading: the rise of education and literacy but also, crudely speaking, a general political consensus that literacy strengthened nationhood and the economies of competing European nations. By the turn of the century the newly independent United States of America opened up as a rapidly growing and particular market. Literacy rates in some areas of the United States were more impressive than anywhere else in the world.

In the decade between 1787 and 1797, 84 per cent of New Englanders and 77 per cent of Virginians signed their wills; a crude measure of literacy, of course, but significantly higher than anywhere else. At the turn of the century in Canada more women could read and write (89.6 per cent) than could men (88.4 per cent).

So what was this ever-growing audience of readers reading, and what difference did it make to those readers? They were reading newspapers and journals, sermons and manuals—but above all novels. A graph produced by the English Short Title Catalogue of the British Library shows the meteoric rise of novel reading (see Figure 9). Poetry and theatre are still popular as are sermons and other religious tracts, histories, and books of instruction. These too are on the rise—but overtaken by far by the novel.

The novel, as a genre, is often seen as the culmination of a story-telling tradition that begins in the oral cultures of

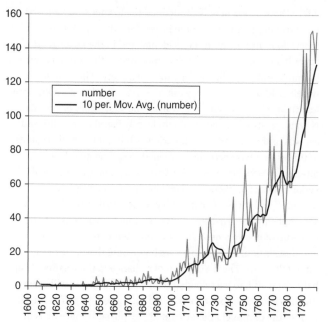

9. **Numbers of titles per year the ESTC has categorized as 'fiction'
(1600–1799).**

the earliest civilizations. The earliest novels of Greece and Rome
are believed to be closely based on stories that had long circulated
within oral traditions. What was new, whether in 12th-century
Japan or medieval Europe, was that the story, or romance, created
a world in which individuals made decisions about their own lives,
and in which intimate feelings were expressed. New notions of
proper behaviours were also germane to these stories, notions of
gallantry—as opposed to heroism—for example.

But can we define what a novel is? The novelist Walter Scott made
an important distinction between the 'romance', also a long prose
narrative, and the novel. The romance is the more obvious
continuation of oral story-telling traditions, whereas the novel

offered something new. Scott defined the former as 'a fictitious narrative in prose or verse; the interest of which turns upon marvellous and uncommon incidents', and in the novel, on the other hand, 'the events are accommodated to the ordinary train of human events and the modern state of society'. The romance is widely held to be a written work of prose narrative of a substantial length, its size distinguishing it from the short story or novella. Novels are also fictional, no doubt largely based on real life and aspects of the author's own experience, but not truthful accounts of things that have actually happened to real people. They are often supposed, however, to be 'true to life', and the degree of verisimilitude, or likeness, to real life has frequently been proposed as a measure of a particular novel's degree of accomplishment. Novels are often assumed, erroneously, to be made up of heterogeneous constituent elements: plot, characters, and description, for example. Distinguishing these, however, is often fallacious. The description of a change in the weather, from balmy and still, to overclouded with a cool wind, say, will often introduce an atmosphere of foreboding, a presaging of a sinister turn in the plot. A character's mood, the physical space he is in, and an early indication of the direction of the plot have all been described—simultaneously.

So much for the typology of the novel as a genre. What about its past? One remarkable facet of the novel is its continuous history. At no point has the novel died out to be reborn after any significant interruption. There were novels in ancient Byzantium, and in ancient Greece and Rome. In the ancient world, however, novels were read aloud in groups. And group reading of the novel is another aspect of it. Novel reading as a private, if not secret, activity is a relatively late innovation in the history of the novel. The earliest novels are usually cited as Petronius' *Satyricon* and Chariton's *Callirrhoe* (both middle of the 1st century CE), Achilles Tatius' *Leucippe and Clitophon* (early 2nd century CE), Apuleius' *The Golden Ass* (middle of the 2nd century CE), Longus' *Daphnis and Chloe* (2nd century CE), Xenophon of Ephesus' *Ephesian Tale* (late 2nd century CE), and Heliodorus of Emesa's *Aethiopica* (3rd century CE). These are essentially stories of heterosexual romantic love between a virtuous woman and admirable man. The conventional morality of these early novels has led some scholars to suggest that these survived—where others may have been lost—precisely because of their acceptable plots which conform to Christian expectations of the virtuous.

In the touching story of Daphnis and Chloe, for example, the eponymous hero and heroine have both been abandoned at birth, independently, and left on a Greek hillside with only some identifying tokens. Daphnis is found by Lamon, a goatherd, who takes him in; Chloe is discovered by Dryas, a shepherd, who decides to take care of her. They are both brought up near the town of Mytilene, unaware of each other's existence, both herding their adoptive parents' flocks. The mischievous god of love, Eros, decides to intervene and engenders in both a powerful love for the other, although neither can understand the passionate feelings they are suddenly beset by. A wise cowherd, however, Philetas, counsels them that the only cure for their overwhelming feelings is kissing. This they do. Lycænion, a woman from Mytilene, then initiates Daphnis into the art of love-making. But Lycænion has warned Daphnis that Chloe's first sexual experience may not be altogether pleasurable for her, in fact it may be painful and bloody. For these reasons Daphnis resists making love to her. The love of the young couple provides the frame for the novel. Within it, briefly, are tales of attempted and successful abduction (of Chloe), and Pan's rescue of her. Daphnis suffers similar trials: he is assaulted and abducted by pirates, and narrowly escapes rape. At the end, both Daphnis and Chloe are recognized by their biological parents, marry each other, and live happily ever after in the countryside.

Longus' story is original only in its formal composition. Its constituents, the good and aggressors, premonitory dreams, and the sudden interventions of the gods, are all familiar aspects of the Greek oral tradition. But Longus' handling of these elements transforms them into a story complete with subtle irony and properly convincing insight into young love and sexual naivety.

Works in Sanskrit from the 6th or 7th century, and the 11th-century Japanese work *Tale of Genji*, are also early precursors, or instances, of the novel. Arabic and Chinese novelists also contributed to the genre in its infancy. *Tale of Genji* (1010), attributed to Murasaki Shikibu, is often considered the first proper novel because of its psychological insights and degree of character development. But any discussion of the work needs to take into consideration its existence in some eighty-eight different editions. Its translations into English are myriad, testifying to the novel's ambiguities and 'literary' status.

Tale of Genji was written by a woman for a female audience within a very particular and highly controlled reading culture. It depicts highly respected courtiers during the Heian period (the last division of classical Japanese history, 794–1185) and provides a window onto the lives of women whose lifestyles are remote. Its language is archaic and its poetic style adds to its strangeness. All this makes it virtually unreadable to Japanese readers—let alone foreign readers—unless they are scholars of Japanese literature.

It was not until the early 20th century, when the history of Japan's literary culture became of interest outside scholarly contexts, that *Tale of Genji* was translated into modern Japanese. The first English translation was made in 1882, but was generally considered to be second rate. The extent to which a poor translation makes a work belonging to a remote cultural tradition accessible to a new readership is questionable, but the role of translation, particularly in relation to the emerging modern novel, is a crucial one in terms of audience, and international literary influence.

Tale of Genji is a highly poetic work. It serves as a reminder that elsewhere in the world epic poetry developed elements that would transfer to the genre of the modern novel. These are essentially the fundamentals of story-telling, in this case, the life and loves of Hikaru Genji, his exploits, his ambitions, his regrets, and those of later generals like himself, his grandson in particular. The plots of many of these epics became the plots of modern European novels. Another early celebrated example is the Arabic tale *Hayy ibn Yaqdhan*, usually translated as *The Improvement of Human Reason: Exhibited in the Life of Hai Ebn Yokdhan*; the plot re-emerges in later novels. The work includes 'An appendix, in which the possibility of man's attaining the true knowledge of God, and things necessary to salvation, without instruction, is briefly consider'd'. It was written in the 12th century by Ibn Tufail, also known as Aben Tofail or Ebn Tophail.

The story may sound slightly familiar. It tells of a feral boy, Hayy ibn Yaqzan, who grows up alone on a tropical island, cared for by an antelope who has adopted him, providing milk and food as he grows. He learns from direct sensory experience, as the animals and birds around him learn. Somewhat improbably perhaps, he makes shoes and clothes for himself and studies the island in all its variety, complexity, and interdependence and so, through reasoned enquiry, he gains wisdom. He lives a disciplined life and forbids himself from eating meat, the flesh of his fellow creatures. When he has reached mature adulthood he meets Absal, a castaway seeking refuge on the island. Absal has grown up in society and their conversations allow Hayy to gain further wisdom into the nature of human existence. In discussing formal religion, Hayy concludes that acquisitiveness, and figurative language (metaphor in particular), may be necessary aspects of organized religion for the common run of men, but that they are distractions from ultimate truth and ought not to be necessary to those who have found true faith independently.

The Improvement of Human Reason: Exhibited in the Life of Hai Ebn Yokdhan belongs within a complex of works which it inspired—either refuting Ibn Tufail's arguments, or influenced by them. A Latin translation of the work, *Philosophus autodidactus*

(*The Self-Taught Philosopher*), was published in 1671, by Edward Pococke the Younger, making it available to a new international scholarly readership. The first English translation was published in 1708, making it known to a still wider readership. These translations are often cited as probable sources of inspiration for Daniel Defoe's *Robinson Crusoe*, which shares the idea of the spiritual growth of a castaway living alone on a desert island. Ibn Tufail's novel has also been linked to fundamental thinking in Western philosophy, for example John Locke's idea of the *tabula rasa* or 'blank slate', the notion that we are born with no innate knowledge but learn solely from perceptual experience. Locke explored these ideas in his famous *An Essay Concerning Human Understanding* (1690) which, crudely speaking, forms the basis of the Western idea of 'empiricism'—all knowledge is based on lived experience.

The Improvement of Human Reason: Exhibited in the Life of Hai Ebn Yokdhan attained best-seller status (an anachronism as the term is a late 19th-century one) in Western Europe during the 17th and 18th centuries, while at the same time profoundly influencing classical Islamic philosophy. The most popular titles before the 19th century would reach maybe 20,000 readers in the weeks immediately following publication. Some intellectual historians have gone further, arguing that Ibn Tufail's novel is a foundation stone of both the modern scientific revolution and the European Enlightenment, informing works of authors as diverse as Thomas Hobbes, Isaac Newton, and, more daringly, Immanuel Kant, who argued that it is our mental structures that provide the structure of human experience. Other European writers who have been cited as the intellectual descendants of Ibn Tufail include Gottfried Leibniz, Robert Barclay, and Voltaire, one of the key spirits of the European Enlightenment.

This great revolution in human thinking was inextricably bound up with the rise of novel reading. The phenomenon was international, often based on translation, much more widespread, and involving a wider social mix of readers than any earlier writing form in human history. Most importantly, perhaps, novel-reading led to lively discussion, heated debates, and controversy. Reading was no longer principally a source of information, inspiration, entertainment, and distraction, but the catalyst for conversation and discussion. In China, the move from the countryside to the city, combined with developments in printing, account for the fact that it was here that oral story-telling first made its way into print. This was during the long Ming dynasty (1368–1644), well over a century ahead of similar changes on the European reading scene.

In Europe, the rise of the modern novel found an audience already accustomed to reading fiction in the form of the 16th-century chapbook, although the term 'chapbook' was coined in the 19th century and used retrospectively. These were cheaply produced and inexpensive, usually printed on a single sheet folded into a small book of between eight and twenty-four pages. Block-printed woodcut illustrations were sometimes included. The reading material printed included folk tales, nursery rhymes, religious stories and moralizing tracts, children's stories (including fairy stories and ghost stories), ballads, almanacs, and poetry. Chapbooks became increasingly popular in the 17th and 18th centuries. In France these same publications were known as *bibliothèque bleue* (belonging to the 'blue library'), because the first publisher to produce them bound them in blue bindings; in Germany chapbooks were known as *Volksbücher*, 'people's books', i.e. affordable books. Historical material became increasingly popular: ancient and medieval history, and legends. Chapbooks were especially popular among the new literate urban 'middle class'. This readership and its reading material were distinct from *belles lettres* (romances, histories, and religious material), produced in expensive bindings and aimed at the gentry and emerging moneyed classes.

Chapbooks were sold on the streets by printer-publishers and book pedlars and encouraged new reading classes, both adult and children. As they were designed to be as cheap as possible to produce and sell, they tended not to last. They were often lent among families and friends and soon wore out. Consequently they are sometimes termed 'ephemera', but they constitute a vital record of reading among large numbers of people. The kind of material published in this format continued to broaden to include short biographies of the famous, and news stories. Gradually the size of editions grew and chapbooks began to be sold wholesale to bookshops. Itinerant vendors, however, still carried chapbooks about with them to sell along with their other wares—haberdashery, condiments, gloves and fans, and other small luxury items otherwise unavailable to rural dwellers. The market was ripe for publications of more substantial proportions.

In his seminal study *The Rise of the Novel* (1957), Ian Watt hypothesized that the major 18th-century works of Daniel Defoe, Samuel Richardson, and Henry Fielding constituted the beginnings of the modern novel. In an earlier draft he had devoted a first chapter to a theoretical exploration of the formal qualities of the modern novel. But he thought it dull to read and lacking in the complete intellectual rigour which he sought in all his writings. So he abandoned the entire chapter and began instead, 'If Defoe, Richardson and Fielding constituted the beginnings of the modern novel…' He claimed that the novel differed in fundamental ways from the prose fiction of their predecessors in particular, in ancient Greece, during the Middle Ages in Europe, or in 17th-century France. In fact the term 'novel' wasn't established as a generic term until the end of the 18th century. Novels by three of the most widely read authors of the 18th century are in part, he argued, the result of changes in terms of access to reading, a new sense of individualism, including economic individualism (crudely each for himself or herself), and of the spread of Protestantism, especially in its Calvinist or Puritan forms. These factors influenced the move to individualize characters—moving away from 'types' or caricatures, and presenting detailed and convincing descriptions of settings and situations, either real or imagined, which could readily be pictured by the reader. Watt sought to demonstrate that biographical, sociological, and historical knowledge explain the *forms* of works of art. This understanding both facilitates the reader's ability to retrieve what the author wrote while at the same time allowing the reader to understand cultural history in a new way. Literature mattered not only because it reflected the *Zeitgeist*—the Spirit of the Age—but also because it in turn became a significant part of cultural and intellectual history exerting a force in its own right.

So what was novel—or new—about the novel? Essentially the novelty was the new 'realism'. During the 1830s, in France, the term 'Réalisme' had been used to draw a distinction between the dominant neo-classical ideal in painting, 'idéalité poétique' ('poetic ideal'), and the new 'vérité humaine' (human truth), exemplified by the Dutch painter Rembrandt (Harmenszoon van Rijn). What mattered, above all, was that the less flattering aspects of human desire and behaviour were now part and parcel of the genre. The fact that Defoe, Richardson, and Fielding were proposed as the first practitioners of the English novel had a good deal to do with the fact that Moll Flanders, Pamela, and Tom Jones, the novels' protagonists, are respectively a thief, a hypocrite, and a fornicator.

Was it that readers wanted to read about characters whose lives were more 'real', or was it that writers represented the world as populated by less than ideal characters, and readers adjusted to the changes? Or had the readership changed so dramatically? More problematically, the modern novel, that is the novel as it came to be in the 18th century, has long been associated with revolutions and the rise of modern democracies. Other changes would include the rise of the use and recognition of irony and sarcasm as narrative modes, and the contemporaneous gradual decline in religious belief, at least of the more fundamentalist kind—that is, reading biblical stories and parables, for example, as literal rather than metaphorical. The rise of the professions, of trained 'middle-class' individuals paid to do a job, also more or less coincides with the rise of a new reading public. Whereas the world of literature had been the domain of *belles lettres*, professional writers and publishers now entered the scene, making their living from their endeavours and consequently fine-tuned to their readers' reading desires.

Other particular claims for the newness of the novel as a particular kind of reading matter have been proposed. Some have argued that the novel genre allows the reader to consider a (fictional) world from a number of different points of view. This 'polyphonic' dimension has been seen as creating, within the novel, an authentic community of equals, which explains an increasingly close association between the novel and the rise and spread of modern democracies.

Reading the novel gave rise to a new sense of individualism. One convincing argument is that certain works of fiction invented individualist characters, able and willing to display wit, will, or energy. These qualities explain their capacity to climb socially, radically changing their social rank. The degree to which they can change their position matches their perceived 'worth'. As soon as novels began to create such exceptional and successful individuals, readers began to understand themselves as individuals with varying degrees of free will and capacities in turn to change their own place in society, to leave one community, for example, and to join another. These ideas are associated with a wide range of particularly influential novelists including Daniel Defoe, Jane Austen, Walter Scott, Charlotte Brontë, Charles Dickens, George Eliot, Thomas Hardy, Rider Haggard, and Bram Stoker. The effect of reading these authors was, arguably, to encourage readers to think of themselves not as immutable individuals but rather as multiple—as a range of possible selves.

So there are two key questions about the novel when in the ascendant: what were people reading? And how? The second is much more difficult to ascertain and in my view much more important and intriguing. How was the new market-share leader in reading—the novel—read? How 'seriously' was reading taken? How did reading really affect people's ideas, in terms of how they then wanted to live—whether social, religious, philosophical, political, or gender-related or any other of the ways in which reading can inform how we'd like to live? The history of the book can tell us about what was published when, and at what cost. It can tell us about the size of editions and often how publications were disseminated. It can tell us whether or not a title is listed in a library catalogue and how many times, and for how long, it was borrowed. It can tell us—to some degree—about reception; if and when a book was reviewed or discussed and discussions were recorded. But given the very private nature of most novel-reading and the fact that it generally leaves no trace, what can we know about how people read? It's a huge subject; what follow are two particularly striking examples. The first is the startling case of Johann Wolfgang von Goethe's *The Sorrows of Young Werther* (1774). The second concerns the rise of the novel—by women authors—enjoyed by women readers.

In 1774, Goethe published a novel called *The Sorrows of Young Werther*. It is an epistolary novel (i.e. made up mostly of letters), and it is in some ways obviously autobiographical. On 30 October 1772, two years before the publication of the novel, Karl Wilhelm Jerusalem, a friend of Goethe's, shot and killed himself with a pistol borrowed from J. C. Kestner, another of Goethe's friends. Goethe had first met Jerusalem when he was a student in Leipzig and they had become good friends during the summer of 1772, in Wetzlar, central Germany. Needless to say, the tragedy made a profound impression on Goethe, and *The Sorrows of Young Werther* can in some ways be seen as an attempt at vindicating his friend.

Jerusalem's death was presumably discussed by Goethe and other friends. Much of what appears in the fictional Werther's letter of 12 August 1771 in *The Sorrows of Young Werther* may have been a summary of the discussion Goethe himself may have used in trying to make sense of, or even to justify, Jerusalem's suicide. In addition, there are various obvious parallels between Jerusalem's life and Werther's, not least their shared unhappy (and unrequited) love for a married woman. The rest of Goethe's novel is largely from his autobiography. He was passionately attached to Charlotte Buff, later the wife of Kestner, and the letters that Goethe wrote to her bear close resemblance to Werther's to the fictional Lotte.

Werther is the first German novella, or short novel, an important and popular genre particularly in German literature. It was also the first German epistolary novel and the first German work of any kind to make both its author and his country's literature internationally known. Translations soon appeared in France, and England, where twenty-six separate editions (of a translation from the French) were published up to 1800. No less a realist than Napoleon was a great admirer of the story, which he is said to have read seven times, and which he discussed with Goethe when they met in 1808. In Germany the work created a tremendous sensation: within twelve years of its first publication twenty unauthorized editions had been issued. The *Werthertracht* (Werther costume), consisting of blue tailed coat, yellow waistcoat, and trousers with high boots, was adopted everywhere and was worn at Weimar by the court when Goethe went there in 1775. The novel's popularity with its readers explains the extraordinary and intensive merchandizing that went with its publication. Scenes from the novel appeared on special decorated porcelain, fans, and even buttons; silhouettes of 'Lotte' circulated; a perfume was named after Goethe's hero (*eau de Werther*); and the Werther costume appeared all over fashion magazines and books.

Today's readers of the novel may be surprised—and puzzled—by its extraordinary success. It remains a moving and in many ways believable story, but it is difficult to take the excesses of emotional outpourings seriously. *The Sorrows of Young Werther* no doubt needs to be read as it would have been by its first readers—as far as this is possible. It shows us how young men felt and behaved in the 18th century and the way people in the 18th century liked to think that a lover's devotion should express itself.

More dramatic still is the way it was read. It was said that people in many countries were apparently so persuaded by the novel that, if disappointed in love, they imitated Werther's manner of death. According to Goethe, 'My friends... thought that they must transform poetry into reality, imitate a novel like this in real life and, in any case, shoot themselves; and what occurred at first among a few took place later among the general public...' That there was significant imitation of Werther's suicide was never demonstrated conclusively but we do know that various authorities were sufficiently concerned to have the book banned in, for example, Leipzig and Copenhagen.

It is difficult to see how one might ascertain today whether or not there was a sudden rise in the suicide rates of broken-hearted young men in the 18th century, but recent research by psychiatrists suggests there almost certainly is a 'Werther effect' as copy-cat suicide is known in the psychiatric world today. It is evidence of the sinister power of certain kinds of reading—or readers. As a result, many countries have now devised guidelines for the media to follow when reporting suicides. It turns out that it is not the fact of reporting a suicide that can be dangerously influential but the *manner in which it is reported*. Contrariwise, trying to prevent suicide by the manner of reporting has very recently been named 'the Papageno effect', after the character of that name in Mozart's opera *The Magic Flute*. Papageno fears that he has lost his love, Papagena, and is planning his death when he is prevented at the last minute by three child-spirits who suggest that he rings his magic bells to summon Papagena. She duly appears.

So the anecdotal evidence of the suicides provoked by reading *The Sorrows of Young Werther* begins to look more convincing. And recent evidence in psychiatry suggests that the narrative technique of the novel may explain its terrible influence. The letter form of the novel is more peculiar than the term 'epistolary' (made up of an exchange of fictional letters) suggests. Unlike earlier epistolary novels, Goethe's has an original distinction and that is that Werther's correspondent's letters are missing. We only read half the story. So Werther writes to his friend, the pragmatic Wilhelm, but the reader isn't able to see his replies. The reader, therefore, becomes Wilhelm's stand-in.

Eighteenth-century readers would be used to novels with a clear moral message, often articulated by the narrator. But reading *Werther* we are left to guess Wilhelm's responses on the basis of Werther's subsequent letter. Having identified so completely with Werther, readers then have to make sense of the sudden and disturbing suicide which the 'editor' (who appears late on in the book) informs us of at the end.

It is the manner of telling of the tale, not the tale itself, that had such a profound effect on the reader. We're left to try to make sense of it much as Goethe was when Jerusalem shot himself—in real life. We have, to a degree, to tell ourselves the tale. And some young men may well have done this in a way which deepened their own sadness. Others may have constructed a different—and more optimistic—story. Interestingly, as mentioned earlier, it appears to be the manner of the telling of real suicides in the press that has to be so carefully handled in order to minimize the dangers of copy-cat suicide. So, to sum up the answer to the question, 'how was Goethe's book read', we can conclude that it is very likely that some young men—and women—took it extremely, fatally, tragically, seriously. The story of Goethe's *Werther* provides striking evidence of just how historically determined reading is.

How moved were readers of women authors of the same period? Interestingly women authors were writing, more often than not, in reaction to their own reading. They provide us with intriguing insights into the 'how' of how some women at least read in the

18th century. Reading, we are reminded, is, of course, the *sine qua non* of writing. Authors may write from their own experience, and from their imaginations, but they also write as a function of their own reading. This may be more or less conscious and in the case of 18th-century women writers was often very deliberate indeed.

A larger-than-life example of a woman reader who baulked at the male authors she read was Stéphanie Félicité comtesse de Genlis (1746–1830), known as Mme de Genlis. She started life a well-heeled aristocrat and ended it impoverished, in large part because of her belligerent writings, or what were deemed to be belligerent. Like most of her contemporaries her education had been mostly of her own devising. She was a keen reader and early on in her life this developed into a passionate desire to further women's education. She was also concerned to promote effective ways of enfranchising and empowering women through new ways of learning. She was piqued by her reading of Jean-Jacques Rousseau's much-celebrated educational novel in five books, *Émile: or, On Education*, published in 1762. One of the volumes focused specifically on the education of a girl, Sophie. According to Rousseau's novel, the formation of young women should be conceived so as to maximize men's happiness. Rousseau was explicit about this:

> Thus the entire education of women must be relative to men. To please men, to be useful to them, to be loved and honoured by them, to raise them when they are young, care for them when they are grown-up, to console them, to make their lives agreeable and gentle—these are the duties of women…and this is what they must be taught from childhood.

More infuriatingly, from Mme de Genlis's point of view, Rousseau did not rule out women 'cultivating their minds'; on the contrary, but this was to be done with the exclusive objective of making women better company for their husbands and their social circles. The conversation of women should be, he explained, 'pleasing but not brilliant, and thorough but not deep . . . . When people talk to her they always seem to find what she says attractive.' Clearly women had to be lively and interesting – but not outshine their male interlocutors. They were to demonstrate brightness, but not wisdom. Rousseau based his female pedagogical theories on the dictates of 'Nature', or so he claimed, and it was this ungodly emphasis that led, no sooner were his tomes out, to their banning in both Paris and Geneva. But like so many banned books they quickly became best-sellers, in this case throughout Europe. By the time of the French Revolution *Émile* served as one of the foundation treatises in what developed into a new national lay educational system. During the second half of the 18th century (1751–96) it appeared in no less than sixty-one English editions, making it one of the most read books in England. Only the skeptical philosopher Voltaire was more popular.

Mme de Genlis was both outraged and intrigued by *Émile* and it became one of the main inspirations for her own educational treatise, *Adèle et Théodore*, published in 1782. Tellingly, she placed the girl's name ahead of the boy's in her title. It is unimaginable that a long and detailed work of pedagogy would reach the best-seller lists today but Mme de Genlis's did. Even abroad her work was enormously popular and in England, was almost as popular as Rousseau's and Voltaire's. Mme de Genlis objected to Rousseau's ideological position for a number of reasons. Firstly she rejected his claim that original sin does not exist. But her real objection was to Rousseau's claims for what he saw as the necessary limiting of female education. Snipes are fired at this idea in *Adèle* but in the third volume of her *Veillées du château* (translated in 1784 as *Late Night Tales at the Castle*), her repudiation of Rousseau becomes both forceful and explicit. The *Veillées* became her most commercially successful publication to date. The first print-run of 7,000 copies sold out in only eight days. It was immediately translated with at least sixty printings in France, Britain, America, Germany, Spain, and Italy. What Mme de Genlis had to say about women's education and the ways in which men had sought to limit it was a direct counter to Rousseau and other less well-known male theorists:

> When men condescend, which is very seldom, to employ themselves a little on our education, they wish to give us vague notions, consequently often false, superficial knowledge, and frivolous talents.... A man of letters, whose daughter gives evidence of wit and love of poetry, may be induced to cultivate these talents, but what will be her father's first care? Why, to rob the young scholar of that confidence that inspires fortitude, and that ambition which surmounts difficulties. He prescribes bounds to her efforts and commands her not to go beyond them...[He] traces a narrow circle round his young pupil over which she is forbidden to step. If she has the genius of Corneille or Racine, she is constantly told to write nothing but novels, pastorals and sonnets.

Mme de Genlis was admired on the one hand for her relative religious conservatism but at the same time for the originality of her ideas about education and her equal commitment to the education of both girls and boys. Among her highly original and imaginative innovations was to make the reading—or the acting out, while reading—of short morality plays a key part of her educational method. She believed that this instilled the right values and was also an excellent—and entertaining—way of developing literacy skills. Reading was not just a matter of the correct 'sounding out of words', it needed to be meaningful and appropriately emotionally charged.

Mme de Genlis was not the only woman of the period to concern herself with the relative neglect of women's education. But nobody in the 18th century before Genlis had written new morality plays adapted specifically to the necessities of a young ladies' 'polite' education. On the other side of the channel, the illustrious Mrs Elizabeth Montagu (1718–1800), campaigner, hostess and patron, and a key founding member of the Bluestockings, recommended it enthusiastically to her nieces. It was highly-praised in the *Critical Review*, when first translated in 1781 (*Theatre of Education*), and described as 'peculiarly serviceable to young women, whom they were principally calculated to instruct'.

Just as Rousseau had been an important prompt for Mme de Genlis's writings, so her writing acted as an influential catalyst for other women writers. Maria Edgeworth read *Adèle et Théodore* as soon as it came out, and immediately embarked on an English translation. She was pipped at the post. But she was only one of numerous famous women writers struck by their continental sister. Jane Austen refers to it approvingly in her novel *Emma* and none other than Mary Wollstonecraft read and re-read it while planning *A Vindication of the Rights of Women* (1792).

A very different woman reader-writer of the time was Elizabeth Carter (1717–1806). She too was largely an autodidact although she was fortunate in her clergyman father who encouraged and guided her education. She was more than competent as a reader of several modern languages, as well as Latin, Greek, Hebrew, and Arabic. She was a poet but her major intellectual contribution was as a translator of works that she thought should be made accessible to English women readers who might not have had her opportunities to learn foreign languages. These were not principally entertaining novels. Her great translation was of Francesca Algarotti's *Il Newtonianismo per le dame* (*Newtonianism for Women*, 1737). This was no lightweight work, nor was its translation straightforward. But despite its earnest and slightly misleading title, Carter's translation became an 18th-century best-seller. The gendered title did not deter men, and it became one of the key works to introduced Newtonian ideas to the general public. It is not the intimidating scientific treatise that the title might conjure. Instead it is a lively, albeit long, and entertaining dialogue between a chevalier (cavalier or knight) and a marchioness (la marchesa di E***).

The setting is near Lake Garda, in a magnificent Italian villa. The venue makes possible the instrumental use of mirrors (in the expansive dining rooms), and *trompe l'oeil* (in the villa's glorious picture galleries). The formal gardens with fountains allow for the staging of various aspects of Newtonian optical theories. Thus their light-hearted conversation, even chit-chat, remarkably, explores the physical theories of the nature of matter and light. Some are dismissed as unsubstantiated. By the end of the work the marchioness's earlier skepticism has been replaced by full confidence in Newtonian theory and not just about light, but almost everything else embraced by his wide-ranging philosophy. Algarotti allows for an extrapolation and extension of experimental science into the diverse fields of metaphysics, ethics and political science. At the time Newtonianism was seen as a direct threat to faith. It was quickly placed on the Catholic *Index* (1739). Carter's was the first translation; others followed in English, French, German, and Dutch. But Carter had thereby proved herself to be one of the most discriminating women readers of the 18th century. Translators at the time often provided titles unlike the original. We can assume that Carter translated Allgarotti's as closely as possible because of her belief that women readers, first and foremost, should read Algarotti. The example of Carter is one of many: what women chose to translate gives us a crucial insight into what works they strongly approved and thus wanted to make accessible to other readers, above all women readers whose education, in the majority of cases, made the originals inaccessible.

In trying to understand the nature of women's reading in the eighteenth century we also have the more obvious evidence left by women readers themselves. But how reliable should we take this to be? We have to allow for irony, self-parody, self-dramatization, playfulness and so on. One of the writers to receive enormous amounts of fan mail from women readers was the popular novelist Samuel Richardson (1689–1761). Some were contemporary women writers such as Sarah Fielding, Jane Collier, Elizabeth

Carter, and Hester Chapone. But by far the most important of Richardson's woman 'reader-critics' as we might term them, was one Lady Bradshaigh. She was from a landed family whose fortunes had fallen and then risen again and she was in many ways typical of his female audience. Her education had been patchy and she had no time—or so she made out—for women intellectuals. In this she was characteristic of women of her class.

Lady Bradshaigh's earliest letters to him, in 1748, were anonymous. In wonderfully breathy prose she described her histrionic experience of reading his *Clarissa*—so far:

> Had you seen me, I surely would have moved your pity. When alone, in agonies would I lay down the Book, take it up again, walk about the room, let fall a flood of tears, wipe my eyes, read again, perhaps not three lines, throw away the book, crying out, excuse me, good Mr Richardson, I cannot go on; it is your fault—you have done more than I can bear; [I] threw myself upon my couch.

But we would be naïve readers if we were to take this accusatory account at face value. Elsewhere in the correspondence between Bradshaigh and Richardson we become well-aware of this—and other—woman-reader's tendency to self-deprecate and exaggerate. In a letter to her novelist-idol of 1749 she described herself as 'middle-aged, middle-sized, a degree above plump, brown as an oak wainscot, a good deal of country in her cheeks'. In short she was an unsophisticated country woman. This was the persona she projected. But Richardson took her very seriously—above all when it came to her responses to reading his novels. He circulated their voluminous correspondence among his close friends and he even considered publishing it, claiming that one series of exchanges was 'the best Commentary that cd. be written on the History of Clarissa'.

At the time, the playful epistolary relationship between an author and a woman reader like Richardson and Bradshaigh was by no means unusual. Alexander Pope (1688–1744) exchanged letters with a remarkable number of women readers many of whom were direct in their praise or criticism of his work, in particular his portrayal of his heroines and women characters. Another important example is Henry Fielding's sister Sarah, herself a novelist. She was far and away her brother's most important sounding-board. She may well also have written work attributed to him. This too was far from uncommon at a time when women writers were often vilified.

For over twenty years Jonathan Swift regarded his reader Esther Johnson, 'Stella', as 'his most valuable friend'. Between 1710 and 1713 he wrote a famous series of letters to her, later published as *The Journal to Stella* (in Richard Sheridan's edition of 1784) in which his debt to her is clearly acknowledged: Swift constantly asks her for her impressions of his latest writings. In myriad ways, women readers exerted considerable and direct influence over what men wrote. They were not the passive, impressionable readers that some have cast them as, soaking up their reading like inanimate sponges.

The newfound confidence, often disguised in myriad ways, of many 18th-century women readers gave rise to the inevitable criticism of men very early on. Figures like the Earl of Shaftesbury (1671–1713), statesman, politician, philosopher, and highly influential writer, sounded alarmist warnings. He crusaded vigorously against the modern novel in particular because of its dire effects on women readers above all, whom he deemed wholly uncritical in their reading. In his work *Soliloquy, or Advice to an Author* (1710), he criticized contemporary writers as unashamedly calculating and flirtatious in their schemes to win over their readers, particularly women readers. In typically vivid prose he likened their writings to 'poisonous fungi, edifying mushrooms, fancy clothes and fancy fictions'. It was not unusual to appeal to the idea of the novel as 'toxic', nor was it original to propose the novel as a deceit, encouraging deceit; the idea of the novel as a fiction or disguise encouraging the disguise of its readers with clothes and manners similar to those of a social group to which they did not belong. In short the novel was encouraging readers to act out their own fictions. The novel was putting ideas into women readers' heads (and into the heads of the less than privileged). And these ideas were above their station. Novels, in short, far from being a harmless escape, were a threat to the *status quo*.

Chapter 5
Forbidden reading

Book burnings

Censorship, book burnings, and secret reading highlight the relationship between reading and power, and hence the relationship between limiting access to reading and political control. But from the very beginning there have been dissidents who refused to give up the intellectual freedom provided by their reading in the face of despotic regimes. Ovid provides an early example. Later, when Christianity became the state religion in Rome, Emperor Constantine tried Arius and the Council of Nicæa banned his doctrine and ordered that the Arian 'sect's' books be burned. The Nazis famously burnt books. The novelist E. M. Forster, in one of his anti-Nazi broadcasts of 1940, used book burnings in Berlin as symptomatic of their whole enterprise. Of these he said, 'The Nazis wished it to symbolise their cultural outlook, and it will. It took place on May 13 (*sic*), 1933. That night twenty-five thousand volumes were destroyed outside the University of Berlin, in the presence of some forty thousand people. Most people enjoy a blaze, and we are told that the applause was tremendous' (see Figure 10).

An ironic editorial in the *New York Times*, in April 1941, also made book burning central to its argument. It is worth quoting

10. Nazi book burning.

at length because it is also a catalogue of book destruction through history:

> And yet, despite the fine record of the German war machine in destroying other people's libraries, it cannot hope to compete, for permanent results, with earlier achievements in the same field. When the Arabs destroyed the Alexandrian Library or, before that, when the goths and the vandals sacked the cultural centres of the Roman Empire, the lost treasures were permanently lost. To replace the lost books at Louvain or Warsaw is merely a question of money to buy new copies.
>
> The art of printing stands in the way of Hitler's plans for the human spirit. The books thrown on Nazi bonfires soon after Hitler's arrival in power were only a symbolic gesture. There were plenty of copies outside of Germany, or for that matter hidden away in the Third Reich. Hitler's only hope of uprooting anti-Nazi culture must be by conditioning the minds of the subjugated peoples so as to immunise

them against the printed word. His serfs must be completely sterilized against the impact of dangerous thoughts, as his Axis friends in Tokyo call them.

Book burnings were also a potent form of protest against the cultural impositions in the colonial world. Students at Farouk University in Alexandria (again) protested against British rule by burning English textbooks. And for some writers having had his or her book burned is a badge of honour, an accolade that proves the writer's desire to resist oppression. The same is sometimes true of having been the subject of an inquisitorial process. Muslims around the world burned copies of Salman Rushdie's *Satanic Verses*. The Harry Potter books were burned in parts of the United States where fundamentalist Christians claimed that they would encourage witchcraft. Most recently, the young schoolgirl Malala Yousafzai was shot in the head, in effect because she read books and advocated girls' literacy on a blog, in a Taliban-controlled part of Pakistan. Dissident book groups, often made up of women, have persistently read in parts of the world where oppressive regimes try to control women's reading.

In the mid-17th century, during the English Civil War, the 20th-century Argentinian writer Jorge Luis Borges reminds us, it was seriously suggested that the entire contents of the archive of the Tower of London be burned, so that every memory of the past be obliterated, in order that a whole new way of life should be initiated. The destruction of books by fire is the most dramatic and spectacular way of preventing certain reading materials from being read. During the Cultural Revolution in China, millions of rare books were allegedly pulped, rather than burnt, in order to be recycled to provide paper for the printing of Mao's *Little Red Book*. This is a process of metamorphosis. Book burnings, on the other hand, are often public spectacles and bring about a total destruction with associations of 'renewal' and 'cleansing'.

The history of book burnings is probably as old as literacy itself. Library collections and their architecture were purposefully burnt in classical times. In 221 BCE, there are records of a library being burnt in China. This was an attempt to destroy the Confucian classics. It failed because learned men had committed them to memory. The burning of the Library of Alexandria in 642 CE by the Caliph Omar may be apocryphal, but it has the status of a foundation myth of book burnings as a pragmatic, but equally symbolic, event. This is the story: after the fall of Alexandria, John the Grammarian, an unfrocked priest, sought an interview with the Caliph and asked for the unwanted books in the library. The Omar's alleged response was this: 'Touching the books you mention, if what is written in them agrees with the book of God, they are not required; if what is written in them disagrees, they are not desired. Destroy them therefore.' In some accounts the books were apparently used as fuel in the city's bathhouses for months. In the Caliph's eyes reading material was an unnecessary distraction from fundamental beliefs and should be done away with in one great pyre.

Repressive political regimes, and religious authorities, maverick leaders, and individuals, have all burned reading material. In early modern France book burning became a secular, rather than a religious, vogue. Voltaire's books were burned in Paris and Geneva.From the mid-17th century until the late 18th century some 1,000 people were imprisoned in the Bastille because of their involvement with the book trade.

In England during the early 16th century crown-sanctioned book burnings were common and royal pyres continued to provide public spectacles well into the 17th century. Reformation theologians' works were burned. Martin Luther's works were set alight in London in 1521 and William Tyndale's vernacular translation of the New Testament a few years later. Tyndale himself was condemned as a heretic by Henry VIII and was burnt at the stake in 1536. It was John Milton who famously made the connection between the destruction of reading material and the destruction of men, writing in his *Areopagitica* (1644), 'as good almost kill a man as kill a good book'. Milton was opposed to all forms of censorship, arguing, as many have since, that a bad book may be no more than 'dust and cinders' but that they should not be destroyed as they might 'polish and brighten the armoury of truth'.

It is an irony that books do not actually burn very easily. As the 19th-century bibliophile John Burton Hill wrote, laconically:

> In the days when heretical books were burned, it was necessary to put them on large wooden stages, and after all the pains taken to demolish them, considerable readable masses were found in the embers; whence it was supposed that the devil, conversant in fire and its effects, gave them his special protection. In the end it was easier and cheaper to burn the heretics themselves than their books.

In the 20th century book burnings have played a role in ethnic cleansing. In Serbia, in 1991 the Albanian language was banned as the language of education. In Kosovo, during the last decade of the 20th century, Albanian-language collections were systematically burned. Again the likening of the burning of books to the destruction of a people is obvious.

This aspect of book burning, likening it to the destruction of a people, came to the fore most dramatically under the Third Reich. The 19th-century German writer Heinrich Heine famously wrote in his play *Almansor*, set in Spain at the beginning of the Inquisition: 'Where one burns books, one will soon burn people.' His prophetic vision is often cited in relation to the Nazi book burnings. The Nazi 'bibliocaust', as *Time* magazine called it, began on the Opernplatz in Berlin on 10 May 1933. German student political organizations had planned the event over several weeks. A timber structure had been built piled high with books. Members of the *Sturmabteilung* (known as the SA, 'Assault Division', or Storm Troopers) were present and further entertainment was provided by marching bands. Thousands of students processed into the square with lighted torches. As the pyre caught fire Joseph Goebbels, minister for propaganda and, curiously, an aspiring novelist, delivered his *Feuersprüche* ('fire incantation' or 'fire oath'). 'From these ashes will rise the phoenix of the new *Reich*,' he declared. The books consigned to the flames he described as pacifist, defeatist, and un-German. Twenty thousand volumes of 'offensive' books were destroyed. Any book that was written by a Jewish author, a Marxist, a Communist, a 'decadent', or humanist, was ceremoniously burned. These fires have become symbolic of the savagery of the Nazi regime. All over Germany the Hitler Youth (the Nazi youth association) organized similar events in university cities.

In December 1933 a small group of opponents to the book burnings met to discuss the establishment of an anti-fascist archive and library, the Library of the Burned Books, in Paris. An international committee was formed including well-known writers such as the exiled German author Lion Feuchtwanger, English writer H. G. Wells, and the French Nobel-prize winning author Romain Rolland. The last was appointed honorary president. He was an open opponent of the Nazi regime and, consequently, one of his books was burned. The Library opened on the Boulevard Arago in Paris, in 1934. A Society of the Friends of the Library of the Burned Books was formed in London and a similar library, the American Library of Nazi Burned Books, opened the same year in New York. The main speaker at the official opening was Albert Einstein. A list of 500 titles had been provided by the Paris Library. In 1935 there was a celebration in Paris of the Library's first anniversary. One of the most important speeches was delivered by the German author Thomas Mann. As the historian Matthew Fishburn writes, 'his address reached behind the spectacle [of book burnings] to show that the combination of the politics of distraction and the draconian controls on the press was lethal, compelling the German public to renounce any knowledge of the "real state of affairs" because the conditions for genuine critique had disappeared'.

The destruction of books is often equated with an erasure of memory, the annihilation of what is civilized, a reconfiguring of history. But even in the ancient world there were those who felt the oppressive weight of the writings of the past. Seneca did not lament the destruction of the Library of Alexandria, and neither did Alexander Pope and Jean-Jacques Rousseau. During the European Enlightenment, in particular, a tension began to emerge between those who wanted to hoard the past and those who wanted to be free from its stifling influence.

Inquisitions

The Inquisition was a group of organizations within the Roman Catholic Church, which claimed to provide a legal structure for the condemnation of heresy. It had its origin in 12th-century France, and was formed with the purpose of rooting out religious sectarianism. The Cathars and Waldensians were early groups to be tried. During the 16th century the Inquisition became a much more widespread reaction to the Protestant Reformation and part of the Catholic Counter-Reformation. It spread from France to Spain and Portugal and to their overseas empires in the Americas, Africa, and Asia. There were major Inquisitions in Peru and Mexico, for example. The Iberian Inquisitions were designed to condemn Jewish anusim and Muslim converts to Catholicism. Anusim is a legal category of Jews who were forced to abandon Judaism against their will.

Both these groups were much larger minorities than elsewhere in Europe. While the Inquisition's censorship in the colonies of the Americas was oppressive, it can't compare with the Spanish invaders' destruction of the unique literature of the Maya people. The burning of the Maya Codices in the 16th century was one of the worst criminal acts committed against a people and their cultural heritage. It represents a huge and significant loss to the world heritage of literatures and languages. The Maya people (sometimes Mayans) are a group of indigenous peoples of Mesoamerica (Mexico, Guatemala, Belize, El Salvador, and Honduras).

The Inquisition came to an end in Europe after the Napoleonic Wars, and after the Wars of Independence in the Americas. It survived, however, within the Papal States, where it was renamed the Supreme Sacred Congregation of the Holy Office in 1908, and then the Congregation for the Doctrine of the Faith in 1965. The CDF occasionally issues notifications of books by Catholic theologians that it judges contrary to church doctrine. Galileo's trial by the Inquisition has stimulated a remarkable imaginative afterlife. No other process in the annals of canon or common law has been reinvented with so many meanings, consequences, and hypotheses as Galileo's.

The main facts of his trial by the Inquisition in 1633 are well known. In 1632 Galileo published his *Dialogue on the Two Chief World Systems, Ptolemaic and Copernican*. In the Copernican system, the Earth and other planets orbit the Sun, while in the Ptolemaic system, everything in the Universe circles around the Earth. Pope Urban VIII reacted unfavourably to it, believing that Galileo's discussion of the earth's motion was not only 'hypothetical', but also 'assertive'. In addition, the Pope claimed that Galileo had failed to give appropriate weight to an important anti-Copernican objection. The argument is that as God is both omnipotent and omniscient, He could have created a non-Copernican universe. In spite of the arguments supporting Copernicanism, the Pope maintained, it can never be declared an absolute truth. Urban and Galileo had already debated these questions in 1624 and the Pope had forbidden Galileo from pursuing his thoughts orally or in writing. One of the many curiosities of the trial is that these earlier matters were barely aired. The sentence of 22 June 1633 depended principally on the book's infringement of three enforcements of 1616, when the Congregation of the Index had decreed that Copernicanism was false and untrue to Scripture. All Copernican books had been banned, and Galileo had been required to cease all work on the Copernican doctrine. The injunction—this is contested—also required that Galileo not believe, defend, or teach anything about the manner of the Earth's movement. The Inquisition claimed Galileo to be a heretic, accusing him 'of having held and believed a doctrine which is false and contrary to the divine and Holy Scripture: that…the earth moves and is not the centre of the world, and that one may hold and defend as probable an opinion after it has been declared and defined contrary to the Holy Scripture.'

Inquisitions are, by definition, both theological and legal processes and they are the means by which very large numbers of books and their authors have been condemned in the interests of preventing others from reading works deemed to be contrary to Scripture.

Defined more broadly, inquisitions have taken place and continue to take place in religions other than Roman Catholicism. Although historically and culturally very distinct, comparisons can be made between the Inquisition of the Catholic Church and, for example, the Ministry of Islamic Guidance in the Islamic Republic of Iran. Both share a virulent rhetoric and an extremism. Modern Iranian history is a history of relatively liberal periods followed by zealous clamp-downs. In 1988, Iranian extremists set out to condemn anyone who opposed their own traditional conservative beliefs. The revolutionary courts allowed for trials against those deemed in any way anti-Islamic or immoral. These inquisitions often led to executions. And even today the power of the Iranian authorities is exercised both within and without the Islamic Republic of Iran. The banning of Salman Rushdie's novel *The Satanic Verses* by the Iranian Ayatollah Ruhollah Khomeini is a relatively recent and high-profile example; not least because a *fatwa* was placed on the author's life and the lives of his publishers, which included his translators. In July 1991 the book's Japanese translator was stabbed to death, and in the same month the Italian translator was also stabbed (although he survived). In October 1993 Rushdie's Norwegian publisher was the target of an assassination attempt which he barely survived. In Turkey, his translator was the object of an attack that killed thirty-seven people.

Informal processes not unlike formal inquisitions have also been established to put books and their authors on trial. Azar Nafisi's *Reading Lolita in Tehran: A Memoir in Books*, published in 2003, is the author's account of life in the Islamic Republic of Iran, and in particular her resignation from her university position and decision to read the great works of Western and Persian literature with seven of her students who are invited to her home. Literature is shown to provide the imaginary world into which they can escape both to 'conceal' and liberate themselves from a reality that has been taken from them by the Islamic regime. Nafisi also writes about her life as a professor at Allameh Tabatabai University during a period of political upheaval. What Nafisi chooses to teach becomes a battleground for Islamists opposed to the teaching of allegedly decadent imports, such as Western literature.

In her book, Scott Fitzgerald's *The Great Gatsby* is the subject of a mock inquisition. The trial involves an appointed prosecutor and defence, challenging Islamist students to make the case for why the novel shouldn't be the object of study. The eponymous protagonist, Gatsby, destroys himself in his attempts to re-imagine his past. This bears a striking resemblance to the Islamic Regime, a cabal of Ayatollahs who stifle life in the present by enforcing their own dream of a supposedly collective past. One of her students, Mr Nyazi, confidentially yet respectfully warns Nafisi, 'for her own good', not to teach *The Great Gatsby*. Mr Nyazi objects to the novel's love plot, arguing, 'We don't have time for love right now. We are committed to a higher, more sacred love', by which he means the deification of the Ayatollah. It is Mr Nyazi's criticisms that lead Nafisi to put the book and its author on trial, with Mr Nyazi as prosecutor, Zarrin as defence attorney, another male student as judge, and the class itself as jury. The high court drama leads to Mr Nyazi being outwitted by the rational and more intellectually able Zarrin.

J. K. Rowling and her fictitious character Harry Potter have also been subject to inquisitions and allegations of heresy. Deuteronomy 18:9–12 is frequently cited by Rowling's critics: 'When you enter the land the Lord your God is giving you, do not learn to imitate the detestable ways of the nations there. Let no one be found among you who makes his son or daughter pass through the fire, who practices divination or sorcery, interprets omens, engages in witchcraft, or casts spells, or who is a medium or spiritist or who consults the dead. Anyone who does these things is detestable to the Lord.' Two authors sum up the two sides of the argument, Richard Abanes (an American journalist known for his right-wing views), in his book *Harry Potter and the Bible*, and Nathan Hill (an American novelist) in his article 'Harry Potter and Other Evils, or How to Read from the Right'. Abanes claims that J. K. Rowling's world is not a 'moral' world consistent with Christianity; her novels promote unbiblical values and unethical behaviour. His general position is that 'the morals and ethics in Rowling's fantasy tales are at best unclear, and at worst, patently unbiblical'. Hill wholly opposes these views, arguing that Abanes has misunderstood how fiction is read and understood. Rowling and Harry have been put on trial all over the United States and the novels, at least, have been the object of book burnings by Christian fundamentalists for many of the reasons put forward by Abanes.

Indexes

The ostensible purpose of the original Indexes of the Roman Catholic Church was to prevent the corruption of people's theological beliefs which in the European Middle Ages included allegedly subversive scientific and philosophical ideas. But there is a wonderful irony about indexes of banned books as they can both seek to prohibit certain kinds of reading and facilitate the identification of reading material that runs counter to the beliefs or ambitions of certain authorities, whether it be the Roman Catholic Church, the Nazi Party, or the far right in South Africa. Indexes are also of particular interest to historians of reading.

The earliest Index of banned books may have been the ninth-century *Decretum Gelasianum* (usually attributed to Pope Gelasius I) although it was never officially authorized. The Roman Catholic Church's *Index auctorum et librorum prohibitorum* (Index of Prohibited Books) of 1559 was the first of a large series of lists of banned books issued by the Church. Known as the Pauline Index—the Pope who issued it was Pope Paul IV—it was replaced by the Tridentine Index, ratified at the Council of Trent (now Trento in Northern Italy). Schisms emerged with some arguing that it was unnecessarily restrictive. A new revised Index was published in 1564. This included a seminal description of what the correct reading of Scripture was to be: 'no-one, relying on his own skill, shall—in matters of faith, and of morals…wresting the sacred Scripture to his own senses, presume to interpret the said sacred Scripture contrary to that sense which Holy Mother Church—whose it is to judge of the true sense and interpretation of the Holy Scriptures—hath held and doth hold; or even contrary to the unanimous consent of the Fathers.' This statement is of profound significance to reading, and even more so to women's reading as they were denied access to the Church as scholars or clerics. The description denies every interpretative element of reading and constrains the reader to understand only what the institution of the Church deems to be 'the true sense' of Scripture. The Roman Catholic indexes also included lists of banned reading material that was considered heretical, anti-clerical, or immoral. In all there were twenty indexes, with the final one published in 1948. It was abolished in 1966 by Pope Paul VI.

Indexes are also compiled as acts of protest and remembrance. In 1996 the South African publisher Jacobsen published detailed bibliographical information about all the reading material censored during South Africa's Apartheid regime (1950–94). The punishment for flouting the censorship regime was torture and killing. *Jacobsen's Index of Objectionable Literature* preserves a record of the evils of Apartheid. The regime's primary aim was to prevent the African National Congress, an extra-parliamentary black liberation organization, from circulating material supportive of its own cause and antipathetic to the values and ambitions of the ruling party. But like other repressive political regimes worldwide, they also sought to erase public memory. Every aspect of life in South Africa was affected and the degree to which the regime implemented censorship went beyond published reading material to include the ANC symbol itself, printed on whatever it might be—T-shirts, cigarette lighters, buttons.

A very different kind of index is regularly published by The American Library Association, through its Office of Intellectual Freedom, which maintains statistics on attempts to exercise censorship in public and school libraries in various states. The ALA regularly publishes lists of books which members of the public have sought to have banned. On average, more than a book a day faces removal from US schools and libraries. Books by Chris Crutcher, Robie Harris, Carolyn Mackler, Phyllis Reynolds Naylor, Marilyn Reynolds, Sonya Sones, Justin Richardson, and Peter Parnell are among those currently frequently challenged or banned.

An event that represents an out-and-out critique of indexes of banned books, in this case the Nazi Index, was the 'Tag des freien Buches' ('Day of the Free Books') which took place in Berlin in 1947. This was where Goebbels had spoken passionately at a book burning, referring to the phoenix of the new order that would rise from the ashes of the burnt books. Alfred Kantorowicz, who had campaigned tirelessly against Nazi book burnings, was the moving spirit behind the event that sought to bring together the four German zones, each occupied by one of the victorious powers. It was a celebration of free speech. Kantorowicz also produced a pamphlet for the event and, days later, was given permission by the Americans to publish his anthology, *Verboten und Verbrannt* ('Forbidden and Burned'). Rivalries between the occupying powers continued, however. In the Soviet zone confiscations of books on the index continued. In late 1947 the *New York Times* reported that US funding for publishing in the American zone had dropped to the point where 'Soviet Papers Flood U.S. Zone'. The Military Government responded by earmarking four million US dollars for paper, most of it for the printing of textbooks. Once again reading material was seen as political propaganda.

Censorship

It is a truism that we can only read if we know how to, and we can only read what is available for us to read. In the southern states of America in the late 18th century draconian laws forbade black people (whether slaves or free persons) from learning to read or write. This was largely the case until the South lost the Civil War in 1865. Despite the steady rise in literacy rates over the past fifty years, there are still 758 million illiterate adults in the world and most of them are women, according to UNESCO's Institute of Statistics. This represents the most extreme form of what is, in effect, total censorship, as large proportions of people are disadvantaged by their lack of access to information. For a long time in the history of reading censorship by price was also a powerful factor in preventing certain readers from reading certain kinds of material.

The South-African-born author J. M. Coetzee is one of the most thought-provoking campaigners against censorship. In his book *Giving Offense* he writes:

> The one who pronounces the ban … becomes, in effect, the blind
> one, the one at the center of the ring in the game blind man's buff.
> For a time, until the blindfold that at the same time marks him,
> elevates him, and disables him can be passed on, it is his fate to be
> the fool who stumbles about, laughed at and evaded. If the spirit
> of the game, the spirit of the child is to reign, the censor must accept
> the clownship that goes with blind kingship. The censor who
> refuses to be a clown, who tears off the blindfold and accuses and
> punishes the laughers, is not playing the game. He is a fool because

he does not know himself a fool, because he thinks that, being in
the center of the ring, he is king.

During the first half of the 20th century novels and poems in both
the USA and the UK were subject to stringent censorship in
relation to their representations of sex and sexuality—and the
scatological. At the same time writers attempted to push back the
boundaries in terms of their treatment of these aspects of human
experience. There were celebrated prosecutions—D. H. Lawrence
for his *Rainbow* and James Joyce for *Ulysses*. And incalculable
numbers of literary and other works were subject to editorial
alteration before they were published. The first four decades of the
20th century was one of the most heavily policed periods of
literary censorship. At the same time it was the period in which
writers fought vigorously and largely successfully against the
rights of nation states to control what readers could read.

Censorship is nowhere more rife than when a nation is at war with
an enemy or itself. Newspapers are often faced with a choice:
reporting the news only highly selectively or facing a complete
shut-down. The press may be taken over by a country's new rulers,
forced to become nothing more than the mouthpiece of those in
power. In the years running up to the Second World War, news
outlets were subject to stringent Fascist censorship in Germany,
Italy, Spain, and Portugal. Censorship in the USSR was similarly
draconian. When the war broke out censorship systems were
in place in every country involved. In the United States and
Britain, the US Office of War Information and the British
Ministry of Information respectively censored material and
issued propaganda stories. Military dictatorships have sought to
exaggerate the evils of the enemy and the righteousness of their
own regimes.

Some of the worst examples of rigid press censorship induced
by military dictators in the 20th century were those of Spain
(the Spanish Civil War 1936–9, the regime lasted 1936–75),

Greece (1967–74), Chile (1973–90), and Nigeria (1966–9). Despite countless pleas from the international community, Turkey still maintains strict censorship through the Anti-Terror Act of 1991, under the pretext of ensuring national security against 'the enemy within', that is, the Kurdish minority.

The justifications for censorship range from concerns for national security if inappropriate knowledge is allowed into the public domain, to political expediency, to claims of obscenity (D. H. Lawrence's *Lady Chatterley's Lover*), of religious offence (the case of Galileo and J. K. Rowling), and the need to protect children (Lewis Carroll's *Alice in Wonderland* was at one time banned in both the USA and China). But these are not clear-cut categories.

Colonial governments, such as 18th-century tsarist Russia, and Britain, exercised tight control over political publications. Examples are Russia in the Baltic, and Britain in Australia, Canada, India, and Africa. Books which might encourage subversive thoughts and acts were censored. In Australia, full censorship lasted until 1923, while in South Africa a press law was passed in 1928 to secure a modicum of publishing freedom. Later in South Africa, however, the politics of racial division severely limited press freedom. The total control during South Africa's Apartheid era was only abandoned in the last decade of the 20th century.

A remarkable case of state censorship took place in Iran, in August 2011. The Ministry of Islamic Culture and Guidance, the government department that monitors both literary publications and republications, refused permission for a new edition of Nezami Ganjavi's 12th-century epic poem *Khosrow and Shirin*. The censors took exception to the classic love story's references to wine-drinking and unchaperoned visits between unmarried men and women. But what shocked them above all was the heroine's embrace of a male body—that of her dead husband. Simin Behbahani, one of the country's foremost poets today, wrote, 'In this country, they take a young, poor boy to prison and rape him there.... Is it possible that those able to rape such an innocent and fragile creature can also think one would derive pleasure from embracing a dead body?'

In the People's Republic of China censorship is controlled by the ruling Communist Party. The government's position is that it has the legal right to control publications both paper and electronic. The laws do not, the government argues, contradict the individual's right to free speech. Various organizations that campaign against unnecessarily widespread censorship and fight for free speech, such as The OpenNet Initiative, Reporters without Borders, and Freedom House, have repeatedly classified China's position with regard to censorship as one of the worst in the world.

It is widely believed that authoritarian regimes rigorously control the media. However, 'watchdog journalism' which checks official data, for example, can serve to strengthen the controlling power by providing information that can improve governance. But careful balances need to be struck. If there is widespread discontent and the extent of the dissatisfaction is known, this can lead to coordinated uprisings. However much regimes seek to censor information and other forms of reading material there is always potential for counter-forces. Writers' manuscripts have regularly been smuggled out to be printed abroad. Boris Pasternak's *Doctor Zhivago* (1957), a novel which takes place between the Russian Revolution of 1905 and the Second World War, was smuggled to Milan and published in 1957. It was distributed to the rest of Europe with the help of the CIA. This was an example of *Samizdat*, a Russian term which refers to literature published abroad, often from smuggled manuscripts. It also refers to the dissemination of dissident material among the intelligentsia within the Soviet Bloc during the period after Stalin.

Censored works of foreign literature were translated in order to be read in the Eastern Bloc countries. There were numerous covert publishing operations during both the Soviet and Nazi periods. These countered the ruling powers' propaganda campaigns and attempts at erasure of history. Censorship is also the subject of scrutiny and campaigning by charities and NGOs. In the UK, the Index on Censorship has become a global organization promoting free expression. More surprising perhaps, Feminists Against Censorship was set up in 1989 in response to the National Council of Civil Liberties' condemnation of pornography. Any attempts to prevent people from reading certain kinds of material will always be met by forms of resistance.

Intangibles

Much of what we read has been edited but the ways in which what we read may have been changed are unknown to us. Reading material, whether in print or electronic form, can be made unavailable by all manner of means. In most cases these are overt and leave a historical record. But there are subtler and more covert forms of censorship which are consequently almost impossible to document. Self-censorship is frequent in the media publishing world. The *Newsweek* columnist Jonathan Alter has argued, 'In a tight job market, the tendency is to avoid getting yourself or your boss in trouble. So an adjective gets dropped, a story skipped, a punch pulled ... It's like that Sherlock Holmes story—the dog that didn't bark. Those clues are hard to find.' The head of the Media Access Project claims that self-censorship is not misreporting or false reporting, but rather *not* reporting at all. Self-censorship, it has been argued, is not the product of 'dramatic conspiracies', but simply the culminating point of numerous small, daily, writerly decisions. Journalists want to hold onto their jobs and editors are under pressure to support the interests of the newspaper or other media outlet. In one survey 40 per cent of journalists and news executives reported that they had deliberately engaged in self-censorship by avoiding news stories they thought 'inappropriate', or softening the tone of their articles for one reason or another.

We all practise self-censorship in the sense that there is a good deal of reading material that we decide not to read for one reason or another. And of course there is a case to be made in favour of certain kinds of control in terms of what becomes public knowledge. In his book *Forbidden Knowledge*, Roger Shattuck considers the consequences of a general loss of limits and taboos. 'The principle of open knowledge and the free circulation of . . . all ideas', he writes, 'have established themselves so firmly in the West that any reservations on that score are usually seen as politically and intellectually reactionary.' Shattuck is interested in exploring certain questions rather than providing dogmatic answers: 'Can we decide if there are any forms of knowledge, true or untrue, that for some reason *we should not know*?' 'Is there any existing or hypothetical knowledge whose mere possession must be considered evil *in and of itself*?' As new technologies allow us to access more and more material can even the question—as to whether we should be free to read anything and everything—continue to be considered illiberal or bigoted?

Chapter 6
Making sense of reading

Interpretation

Reading is an interpretative act and this is not simply the case when it comes to what we think of as more complex writing—religious scriptures, philosophical texts, legal documents, or literary works. The simplest language can need interpretation. If, when driving, we see a sign saying 'Heavy Plant Crossing', this minimal communication needs consideration; we need to be able to understand 'plant', in this context, as meaning not a living thing that grows in earth, water, or on other plants, but rather as meaning a large, heavy machine or vehicles used, for example, in road-building. We expect large lorries and earth-movers, not triffid-like monsters.

Hermeneutics is the discipline that concerns itself with the theory and methodology of interpretation. The term is derived from the Greek word ἑρμηνεύω (hermēneúō), meaning simply 'to translate, interpret'. Its history is crucial to the history of reading and brings to the fore the myriad ways in which reading has been understood across time and space. In ancient cultures like those of the Greeks and Romans, civilization itself was deemed to depend on the preservation, interpretation, and communication of key 'authoritative' or 'foundational' writings—religious, philosophical, and literary.

The world view of the ancients was a holistic one, epitomized by the words of Marcus Aurelius (121–180 CE) who wrote: 'All things are implicated with one another, and the bond is holy; and there is hardly anything unconnected with any other thing. For things have been coordinated, and they combine to form the same universe. For there is one universe made up of all things, and one god who pervades all things, and one substance, and one law, one common reason in all intelligent animals, and one truth; if indeed there is also one perfection for all animals which are of the same stock and participate in the same reason.' Everything that was learnt whether from experience, contemplation, conversation, listening, or reading connected into a coherent whole. Reading was primarily a matter of making connections, a harvesting and accruing of knowledge, rather than a critical process of discerning truths amid falsehoods. For a very long period in the Graeco-Judaeo-Christian tradition, science and religion derived from two 'books', both authored by God: the book of the Bible and the book of nature.

'Books', understood both literally and metaphorically, have been central to numerous religions including more modern sects such as the Mormons' *Book of Mormon* (1830), translated by Joseph Smith. It represents the Mormons' 'Bible'. The volume runs to some 500 pages and has never been out of print. It has been translated into more than 100 languages. Its 100 millionth copy was published in 2000. Within the Abrahamic religions—Judaism, Christianity, and Islam—the 'Book' and how it is read is central. These faiths depend on an understanding of religious belonging and living based on divine revelation as written in sacred texts. If this is the case, however, how does this square with hermeneutics? If God has dictated *directly* to a prophet or an apostle, how, then, can interpretation be necessary? This is where religions essentially divide into, crudely speaking, fundamentalist and, say, liberal. Jewish traditionalists hold that the Hebrew Bible (the *Torah* or *Pentateuch*) was dictated by God directly to Moses although this does not mean that all traditional Jewish scholars deny the need for interpretation. Likewise, in the Muslim religion, the Koran is explicitly described as the directly dictated words of God but is nevertheless subject to interpretation according to liberal Muslim scholars who read the Koran independently of clerical authority and established reading traditions.

The relationship between reading and the Buddhist tradition stands apart (as does Christianity), as unlike Hinduism (and Sanskrit), Islam (and Arabic), and Judaism (Hebrew), Buddhism (and Christianity) have highly complex multilingual histories. The life of Buddhism has been culturally and geographically dispersed and, historically, embraced numerous languages, including for example Pāli, Tibetan, Sanskrit, Chinese, Korean, and Japanese. Nor does Buddhism have one principal text that contains the religion's essential tenets. What we know as Buddhism today is a diverse collection of different philosophies and schools of thought, ranging from Bahuśrutīya, one of the early Buddhist schools, to Zen, a well-known branch of Mahayana Buddhism that originated in Tang China.

A further distinction between Buddhism and other religions arises from a distinct notion of reading's relationship with religious belief. Koans provide a useful example. These are riddle-like, sometimes paradoxical questions which stimulate spiritual understanding. A well-known koan is about hands clapping and the sound one hand might make. The 'answer' doesn't arise as a function of analytical reasoning. The solution to a koan comes with the abandonment of the rational in favour of the intuitive. The first collection of koans was made in the 11th century CE. They are a favourite teaching tool of the Rinzai school of Buddhism.

Similarly the truths of Zen cannot be learned by reading particular texts. Buddhism's relationship with the practice of reading is at the meditative extreme. It is a free-wheeling, interactive, and inwardly reflective practice. The discipline of hermeneutics, or the science of interpretation, meets its toughest challenge in certain Buddhist reading practices.

In Western philosophy on the other hand, hermeneutics may be defined more broadly as the study of human understanding. The new digital technologies have vastly added to and in many ways transformed the way we gather knowledge, and this change in the reading landscape is unprecedented in human history. The internet is the most powerful and heterogeneous tool ever invented to spread education. But the fact that reading no longer takes place principally within a community—the family that has provided the books, or schools, or local libraries, and so on—has created what some see as an intellectual crisis. The 'infotainment highway' provides access to material which cannot easily be recognized as fact or fiction. In other words there is a danger that we no longer know quite *what it is* that we are reading. This is the *sine qua non* of hermeneutics; without a *context*, there can be no intelligent—or useful—interpretation.

Rhetoric

Reading is inextricably bound up with writing, and writing with speech and rhetoric. Speeches, and anything that is written, are written for a purpose. That's why there is an intimate and fascinating relationship between rhetoric and reading. Plato famously defined rhetoric as the 'art of enchanting the soul'. And this idea of magic or enchantment accounts for the suspicion often associated with it. Today rhetoric is mostly used as a critical term associated with political spin and empty promises. The derogatory meaning implies an eloquent, elegant, or ornate use of language, calculated to persuade—irrespective of the truth. Used pejoratively it is language characterized by artificial, insincere, or ostentatious expression. While the derogatory meaning only comes into the language in the 16th century, suspicion of rhetoric has a longer history. It was in 5th- and 4th-century BCE Athens and in 1st-century Rome that the idea of codifying persuasive language into an 'art' was first conceived. Cicero's manual *On Invention* (84 BCE) is a handbook for orators. It was originally made up of four books, but only two have survived. Cicero is not uncritical of the potential risks of rhetoric. At the same time he regards the discipline as contemporaneous with the beginning of civilization.

Rhetoric is in some ways about debate and its validity has given rise to controversy from the beginning. The fundamental question at the heart of this dispute is simply whether rhetoric is a means to an end, the end being knowledge, or whether it is merely an art or a skill that sets out successfully to persuade, regardless of the truth. As modern readers, particularly of the media and political writings, we are often prompted to consider the same question. This reaches a tipping point in 2016 when, after much debate, the *Oxford English Dictionary*'s Word of the Year was announced to be 'post-truth', defined as, 'relating to or denoting circumstances in which objective facts are less influential in shaping public opinion than appeals to emotion and personal belief'. And those appeals, if successful, will depend on the skilful use of language, or rhetoric, because it is the rhetorical strategies of the writer which control, to a large extent, the engagement of the reader.

Translation

The relationship between reading and translation is multifarious. Most obviously, translation can make reading material available to a readership ignorant of the language of the original text. This process is as old as literature itself. There are fragments of translations of the Sumerian *Epic of Gilgamesh* into the languages of south-west Asia from the second millennium BCE. But the degree to which reading a translation can be likened to the experience of reading the original is obviously questionable. The cultural and linguistic context in which a piece of writing comes into existence fundamentally affects how it is read.

Translation has been of paramount importance to the spread of world religions and, contrariwise, the challenging of organized religions. When missionaries translated the Christian 'Holy Spirit' into indigenous African languages the concept was necessarily 'domesticated' and gained what is arguably a spurious familiarity within a quite different spiritual world for the African worshipper. The feasibility of translation is necessarily bound up with degrees of culture overlap or distance. In an ever-increasingly global world where English as a second language dominates, we need to beware of reducing cultural differences and richness through reductive translation practices. Much of what we read in translation will seem spuriously accessible and familiar.

Political translation movements may be organized attempts to make reading material available that the authorities in a particular society have sought to censor. In the Middle East Muslim clerics had vehemently opposed the printing press for centuries because of its power to spread new ideas and potentially subversive knowledge. But in the 19th century they lost their hold on publishing. In Egypt, for example, between 1880 and 1908, more than 600 newspapers and journals appeared. One of the most successful was *al-Muqtataf*, a journal closely associated with a translation movement that made various canonical works of the European Enlightenment available to Middle Eastern readers, including Montesquieu's *Considerations on the Romans* and Fénelon's *Télémachus*. Montesquieu was an 18th-century French political philosopher and his thesis, in his *Considerations*, was that wealth, and expansionist military ambitions, led not to Rome's ascendancy, but to a weakening of Roman citizens' sense of civic duty which in turn led to the downfall of Rome. For 19th-century Egyptian readers this was revelatory. Fénelon's *Télémachus* is also a didactic work. The novel's hero, Mentor, argues for a new political system, organized on democratic lines with a national government, and a 'Federation of Nations', internationally, to solve disputes between countries. Somewhat simplistically, Fénelon contrasts the wealth and warmongering of Rome with the greater sense of equality of the Greeks. In terms of personal morality, Mentor argues against the ultimately self-defeating ambitions of wealth and self-interest in favour of concern for others. In the late 19th century in the Middle East, these ideas, translated into the Middle Eastern vernaculars, were revolutionary.

Women have often been the fortunate readers of works in translation that would have been unavailable to them in their original languages. Lucy Hutchinson's translation of the Roman poet and philosopher Lucretius in the 17th century was a remarkable early example. She translated *De rerum natura* (*On the Nature of Things*) in 1675. It is a 1st-century BCE didactic poem which explains Epicurean philosophy for a Roman audience. Most importantly, Lucretius explores the ideas of atomism, or the nature of the mind and soul, and the origin of the world and universe. Crucially, Lucretius argues that the world is controlled by physical principles, guided by *fortuna* ('fate'), and not the divine intervention of the traditional Roman gods. Lucretius' emphasis on the pursuit of pleasure was condemned by 17th-century puritans. For a woman to undertake a translation naturally raised eyebrows.

In 18th-century Europe women benefited from an explosion of translations from Latin into the vernaculars. Elizabeth Carter, a highly educated clergyman's daughter, set about translating works to which she felt women readers ignorant of the classics or the European languages should have access. A best-selling example of her work was *Newtonianism for Women* (1737; see Chapter 4), a translation of Francesco Algarotti's *Il Newtonianismo per le dame*.

The process of translation raises all manner of theoretical questions. The ancient Greeks discussed questions of literal (metaphrastic) and idiomatic (paraphrastic) translation, and these two concepts continue to dominate translation theory. Cicero and Horace, in 1st-century Rome, were among the first to criticize translation based on a *verbum pro verbo* (word-for-word) approach. And there have been many arguments for the impossibility of real translation. Roger Bacon, the 13th-century English intellectual, argued that for a translation to be true, the translator must have a profound knowledge of both the language he is translating from and the language into which he is translating. In addition, he must fully understand the science, in Bacon's argument, that the text discusses. Given that such intellectuals were as good as non-existent, he called for the abolition of all translation. The French writer, politician, and diplomat François-René de Chateaubriand, often considered the founder of French Romanticism, claimed that *literary* translation was an impossibility:

> In a living literature, no-one is a competent judge except of those works in his own language. You believe in vain that you possess instinctively a foreign idiom, someone else's breastmilk... The more intimate, individual, national the talent, the more its mysteries elude the mind that is not a *compatriot* to this talent... Style is not cosmopolitan like thought: it has its native land, a sky, a sun all of its own.

There is however a general consensus that original or inventive texts, whether scientific, philosophical, theological, and so on, can be translated without significant loss of their originality or inventiveness. The degree to which this is true of literary inventiveness is a matter of widely varying views. The Russian-born linguist and semiotician Roman Jakobson, in the late 1950s, in his seminal paper 'On Linguistic Aspects of Translation', declared that 'poetry [is] by definition untranslatable'. The novelist and translator Vladimir Nabokov shares Jakobson's position and, like many translators of poetry, considered rhymed, metrical, versed poetry to be in principle untranslatable. For this reason he rendered his 1964 English translation of Alexander Pushkin's *Eugene Onegin* in prose. The reading experience of formal poetry is clearly quite different from that of prose.

Still more extreme positions have been adopted. The French writer and philosopher Jean-Paul Sartre, in his famous essay 'What is Literature?', argued that reading is itself a 'reinvention'. This is tantamount to understanding reading as itself a form of translation. Translation is, in a sense, simply the record of a unique—if particularly thorough—reading experience. The French theorist Roland Barthes continued in this theoretical tradition, arguing that 'the goal of literary work (of literature as work) is to make the reader no longer a consumer, but a producer of the text'. The choices which are integral to the reading of a complex text require the reader to reassemble, in effect, the words on the page according to his or her own understanding of its meaning. Reading becomes an individualistic creative process and not one of uncritical absorption of another's creation.

The contemporary American writer and translator Eliot Weinberger, famous for his translations of the Nobel Prize-winning writer and poet Octavio Paz, Mexican poet and diplomat, has proposed a similar argument: 'Every reading of every poem, regardless of language, is an act of translation: translation into the reader's intellectual and emotional life.' As our intellectual and emotional lives are in constant flux, he goes on to argue, 'the same poem cannot be read twice', as our engagement with the poem will vary according to current preoccupations and mood. Weinberger explains:

> In its way a spiritual exercise, translation is dependent on the dissolution of the translator's ego: an absolute humility toward the text. A bad translation is the insistent voice of the translator—that is, when one sees no poet and hears only the translator speaking.

And he reminds us, near the end of the collection: 'The point is that translation is more than a leap from dictionary to dictionary; it is a re-imagining of the poem.' As no individual reader remains the same, each reading becomes a different—not merely another—reading. This idea is nowhere more convincing than when it comes to moving between two fundamentally different languages.

Weinberger's book *19 Ways of Looking at Wang Wei (with More Ways)*, published in 2016, with an afterword by Octavio Paz, is an expanded version of Weinberger's *19 Ways*, first published in 1987. The Chinese poem, by the 8th-century Tang poet Wang Wei, is made up of four lines:

空山不見人，
但聞人語響。
返景入深林，
復照青苔上

Weinberger also provides a transliteration into modern Mandarin, character by character, and seventeen other versions in English, French, and Spanish. The new, expanded edition offers sixteen further versions including three in German. So here we have thirty-five poems, all of which derive from Wang Wei's poem. One of Weinberger's favourites is by an American scholar, Burton Watson:

> Empty hills, no one in sight,
> only the sound of someone talking;
> late sunlight enters the deep wood,
> shining over the green moss again.

So what do these insights into the pluralities of translation tell us about reading? The way a Chinese poem is read is different in various ways from the way a poem in English or another non-character-based language is read. The calligraphy itself is an art form and the internal structure of Chinese characters has an aesthetic appeal of its own. Chinese characters all occupy the same space on the page and, because there are exactly five characters per line, Wei's poem is a neat rectangle. Reading Wang Wei's poem is also *looking at it*. Most celebrated Chinese poets in the early period were also master calligraphers. Wang Wei was as celebrated for his calligraphic hand as for his poetry.

When looking at a Chinese poem the representational dimension of some characters (or ideograms) is recognized by the reader. Even a non-reader of Chinese is immediately aware of various patterns. For example, the simple character 人 at the end of the first line (reading from left to right), which recurs in the middle of lines 2 and 3 (where it gains a horizontal dash at the top), seems almost 'resolved' in the equally simple final character of the poem: 上, an angular slightly embellished version of 人. Reading Wei's poem from top to bottom and left to right, the second character of the first line is a mountain and the last character of the line is a person. Both can be 'read' or 'seen' as abstractions which derive from more literal representations. The American poet Ezra Pound famously saw the fourth character in line one (reading from left to right), as an 'eye on legs'. One translation of the character is 'to see'. A single Chinese character may be a noun, a verb, and an adjective. It may even have meanings that are antithetical. Character 2 of line 3 is both 'fing' (brightness) and 'ying' (shadow), again reading from left to right. How the character is read, or understood, is a matter of context.

Weinberger's experiments with translations of Wei's poem demonstrate his conviction that a successful poem is made up of 'living matter' that 'functions somewhat like DNA, spinning out individual translations that are relatives, not clones, of the original'. Reading poetry, which is often language in its most mobile and multiple form, is an experience, an event, and as such unique. A translation can be no more than the record of one such reading—and sometimes seeing—experience.

When looking at a Chinese poem the representational dimension of some characters (or ideograms) is recognized by the reader. Non-Chinese poets have also sometimes tried to emphasize the visual representation in a poem. The French poet Guillaume

tout terriblement

Guillaume Apollinaire

11. Guillaume Apollinaire, 'Cheval'.

Apollinaire, in his collection *Calligrammes*, provides good examples. Figure 11 shows his poem entitled 'Cheval' (Horse).

Reading the literary

Disagreements about the merits and demerits or the essential meaning of a literary text are all dependent to varying degrees on different readings, while theories about literature are as old as literature itself. But the rise of university education, particularly from the 19th century onwards, institutionalized the study of literature and gave rise to a rapidly growing number of books *about* literature—or reading. Literature is arguably the pre-eminent site for the exploration of reading because of the ambiguities, paradoxes, and complexities of so much of the literary.

Principally in Europe and the USA, the discussion of literature, its strengths and weaknesses, and its demands and delights, underwent a transformation towards the end of the 19th century. What had been essentially lively conversations between well-read gentlemen—and some women and journalists—became a vast profession of large numbers of specialists operating particularly in the universities, and on a worldwide stage.

Modern literary criticism can be explained in part in terms of a rejection of the 19th-century European Romantics' interpretative notion of the pre-eminent importance of the *Volksgeist* (the unique spirit and character of a nation's people) and the *Zeitgeist* (the spirit of the age), which emphasized the cultural and temporal *context*, whether socio-political, economic, or personal, from which the literary work emanated. Two schools of criticism emerged which demonstrate the degree to which questions of *reading* became central to discussions of the literary: Russian Formalism and the Anglo-American New Criticism. These shared a common concern to attribute meaning not to historical context, including the author's biography, and his or her intentions, for example, nor to a set of predetermined values or representational codes to which the work might or might not show allegiance, but to the *form* and *choice of words* on the page; 'close reading' became the name of the game, and remains central to virtually all literary critical and theoretical endeavour today.

Formalism is in some ways a more codified and systematized version of the widespread European belief in 'Art for Art's sake', the common English translation for the French expression 'l'art pour l'art'. The value of art, subscribers to this view claimed, is *intrinsic*. It is divorced from any moral, informative, or practical function. We read for pleasure or to appreciate beauty; we read for reading's sake. This vision of literature's *raison d'être* originated in the efforts of a group of dissatisfied writers and artists who rejected the idea that art should express moral truths, on the one hand, and represent an accepted reality on the other. They also questioned the preconception that art must have a 'subject', or central focus. Instead they highlighted the uniqueness of art as a human product, principally in terms of *form*. Reality, they claimed, was 'formless'; the artwork, on the other hand, created a structured world. It is the distance between the reality of the world and the reality of the artwork that they championed and celebrated and which Formalist critics investigated. Broadly speaking, the writings of the literary modernists, poets like T. S. Eliot and novelists like Virginia Woolf, whose work self-consciously broke with traditional literary compositional techniques, were particularly ripe for Formalist critical approaches. The Formalist's test for the validity of a work of literature, even for its status *as* literature, was that its meaning cannot properly be conveyed except in the language in which it was originally written; any attempt to summarize or paraphrase is no less than a betrayal of the literary text's meaning. Reading the primary literary text itself is without substitute; any simplified version of it is a betrayal. The literary text, the modernists claimed, could no longer be discussed in terms of its expression of a writer's self, or of an age. The text's meaning was no longer outside the text but within it, made up of the words on the page. Literature required nothing more than intelligent careful reading.

The critic's task consequently became one of identifying the text's *literariness*—its linguistic singularity, its stylistic, poetical, or rhetorical features, for example. This kind of textual analysis necessitated a particular kind of reading: one that was multidimensional, rather than primarily linear. Sound patterns in poetry, for example, required a careful plotting of internal as well as end-of-line rhyme. Instead of reading conventionally, line by line, left to right, and down the page, features needed to be considered within groupings which transcended a linear reading, identifying, for example, images shaping a short story or telling symbols accruing during the course of a novel. What mattered, the Formalists argued, was not simply the identification of certain technical literary attributes, but the explanation of how the meaningful whole was made up of these contributing linguistic tropes. What was often discovered was the text's intriguing ambiguities and paradoxes, the play of irony, and so on. And the recurrent identification of these features in different genres from different historical periods led some to question the usefulness of the Formalists' approaches because rather than 'explaining' the literary text, they further complicated it. The more carefully the literary text was read, the more problematic assimilating meanings became. Reading exposed features of texts which required still more rigorous readings.

Some literary critical debate was informed by philosophical perspectives. One of the most important, in terms of reading, is phenomenology. The first major proponent of the perspective was Edmund Husserl (1859–1938). His primary interest was in the idea of consciousness, expectation, or *intentionality*. Consciousness, he argued, was not a mirroring, but a willing. His view can be explained by means of the experiment in *Gestalt* psychology: the mental switch, for example, that turns an image of a vase into an image of two faces, as in Rubin's 'vase' (see Figure 12).

We are aware, Husserl argued, of what it is that we want, and therefore choose to see; in this case, whether the faces or the vase. Both cannot be seen simultaneously: we opt to see one or other. And this same process occurs when we read. We wish or will that something which may be ambiguous 'mean' something specific.

Common sense reading

The value of thorough reading or of extensive literary analysis has been questioned all along by creative writers in particular. Vladimir Nabokov maintained that good readers do not read books, and particularly those which are considered to be 'great', 'for the academic purpose of indulging in generalizations'. Stephen J. Joyce, James Joyce's grandson, claimed, 'If my grandfather was here, he would have died laughing...*Dubliners* and *A Portrait of the Artist as a Young Man* can be picked up,

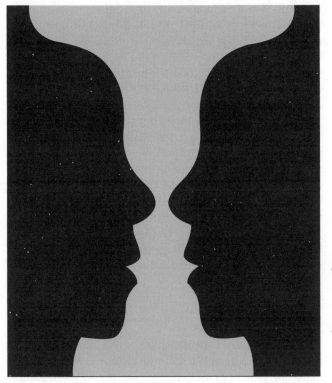

12. Rubin's 'vase'.

read, and enjoyed by virtually anybody without scholarly guides, theories, and intricate explanations, as can *Ulysses*, if you forget about all the hue and cry.' He also later questioned whether anything substantial had been added to his grandfather's literary legacy by the 200 plus books of associated literary criticism stored in the Library of Congress.

More recently literary discussions have broadened so that readings of literary texts are often discussed as cultural products to be considered alongside others: anthropological data, advances within the field of linguistics, travel guides, prison regimes, and school textbooks, for example. The political moment—and particularly ecological and international political crises—also started to concern literary critics. Titles started to appear which suggested that Theory was over: Thomas Docherty, *After Theory* (1990), Benjamin Bennett, *Beyond Theory: Eighteenth-Century German Literature and the Poetics of Irony* (1993), David Scott Kashan, *Shakespeare After Theory* (1999), Valentine Cunningham, *Reading After Theory* (2001), Terry Eagleton, *After Theory* (2003), and many others. But publishers retain a large market for criticism, approaches to, guides to, companions, readers (selections of texts in a particular area), encyclopedias of, and so on. This is not simply because literature can be difficult, but because we will always be interested in other people's readings, just as we are intrigued by our first readings of works we choose to revisit in later life. And in an age saturated with information, readers are intrigued by single-author short guides and introductions.

Rereading

The growing interest in rereading, as a subject, has given rise to accounts which suggest that it isn't simply poetry which is unique in the singularity of its reading experience. The American literary scholar John Kelleher has described his successive readings of James Joyce's autobiographical work, *Portrait of the Artist as a Young Man*:

> I remember that when I first encountered Stephen Daedalus [James Joyce] I was twenty and wondered how Joyce could have known so much about me... Perhaps about the third reading it dawned on me that Stephen was, after all, a bit of a prig; and to that extent I no longer identified myself with him (How could I?) Quite a while later I perceived that Joyce knew that Stephen was a prig; that, indeed, he looked on Stephen with quite an ironic eye. So then I understood. At least I did until I had to observe that the author's

glance was not one of unmixed irony. There was compassion in it too, as well as a sort of tender, humorous pride.

The potential for a work to give rise to distinct and various readings has been identified as a fundamental criterion of any 'classic' work of literature. In the title essay of his book *Why Read the Classics?*, the Italian author Italo Calvino begins his first chapter by putting forward various definitions. The first is: The classics are those books about which you usually hear people saying, 'I'm rereading…', never 'I'm reading…'. At the end of this first section he writes: 'Reading a great work for the first time when one is fully adult is an extraordinary pleasure, one which is very different (though it is impossible to say whether more or less pleasurable) from reading in one's youth. Youth endows every reading…with a unique flavour and significance, whereas at a mature age one appreciates…many more details, levels and meanings.' A further definition proposed by Calvino is this: 'A classic is a book which has never exhausted all it has to say.'

C. S. Lewis, albeit in his old-fashioned way, has this to say about rereading:

> An unliterary man may be defined as one who reads books once only.…We do not enjoy a story fully at the first reading. Not till the curiosity, the sheer narrative lust, has been given its sop and laid asleep, are we at leisure to savour the real beauties. Till then, it is like wasting great wine on a ravenous natural thirst which merely wants cold wetness.

C. S. Lewis was a professor of English at Oxford University and his insights are those of a highly literary man. Roland Barthes, the French writer and intellectual, has a more obvious, and more political, line. He begins by arguing that rereading flies in the face of voracious capitalism: 'Re-reading, an operation contrary to the commercial and ideological habits of our society, which would have us "throw away" the story once it has been consumed ("devoured"), so that we can then move on to another story, buy another book.' He then describes how rereading 'is tolerated only in certain marginal categories of readers (children, old people, and professors)'. The process of rereading, he claims, 'contests the claim which would have us believe that the first reading is a primary, naïve, phenomenal reading which we will only, afterwards, have to "explicate", to "intellectualize"'. Barthes's point is that each and every engagement with a literary text is a unique encounter, and rereading is no exception.

Do we reread a book because we want to replicate the original reading experience we remember, or do we reread knowing that the book will have 'changed'—or rather that we have changed? One of the novelists I reread—and I am far from alone here—is Jane Austen. The success of love-affairs—and Lizzie's above all—was my primary preoccupation when I first read *Pride and Prejudice*. On rereading I delight above all in Austen's manner of telling, the acute irony, Austen's powers of observation which, as a reader, I enjoy viscerally as well as intellectually. This is the passage that now fascinates me:

> 'How despicably I have acted!' she cried; 'I, who have prided myself
> on my discernment! I, who have valued myself on my abilities!
> who have often disdained the generous candour of my sister,
> and gratified my vanity in useless or blameable mistrust! How
> humiliating is this discovery! Yet, how just a humiliation! Had
> I been in love, I could not have been more wretchedly blind! But
> vanity, not love, has been my folly. Pleased with the preference of
> one, and offended by the neglect of the other, on the very beginning
> of our acquaintance, I have courted prepossession and ignorance,
> and driven reason away, where either were concerned. Till this
> moment I never knew myself.'

I think that many women could measure their own growth in relation to their understanding and interest in Austen's novels. Those who are opposed to rereading point out that there is more to be read than can be managed in a lifetime, so why waste important time returning to books that are already known. But the experience of rereading creates a palimpsest of our awareness of ourselves, others, and life. The rereading of a work is informed both by our memory of our first reading and by all the experiences and changes to our consciousness that have taken place during the intervening period between the first and later reading. Rereading is neither a childish regressive practice, nor a luxurious excess, nor a dry academic procedure, but a vital and essential practice if we are to understand the multifaceted activity that reading is—and who we are.

Chapter 7
Pluralities

Readings

Many of us, most of us, spend a very large part of our days reading.
But what we read is in myriad forms. There is surely an argument
for 'reading' to become a plural with a new sense—readings.
On the face of it, one of the apparently biggest changes in relation
to reading is a matter of medium. Most of us spend most of our
time reading electronic or digital media—on our PCs or laptops,
our notebooks or smartphones.

We are not the only readers. Researchers have been working on
machine reading for decades. Optical character recognition or
OCR is highly refined. It involves the mechanical or electronic
conversion of text, whether handwritten, typed, or printed, into
machine-encoded text. It is fundamental to other areas of
development in, for example, cognitive computing (artificial
intelligence (AI) and signal processing), machine translation, text
to speech reproduction. While machine 'reading' in terms of OCR
may already be well developed, machine reading comprehension
remains limited despite heavy investment by companies like
Alibaba and Microsoft. Despite some new successes, Microsoft
posted the following acknowledgement in 2018: 'We are still a
long way from computers being able to read and comprehend
general text in the same way humans can.'

We still read books, but that activity is also increasingly bound up with the electronic. Readers of the novel may read the paperback version, the modern incarnation of the chapbook, or they may read blog fiction, twitterature, as well as the stories that circulate in social media platforms. Much of this could be reproduced in a paper version, but not all of it. Innovations include interactive dimensions, requiring a touchscreen or voice-recognition, for example. The reader is ever more in control—but within certain boundaries. The imaginative re-creation of a world required of the reader of a literary novel is in many ways distinct, but again limited. And just as the novel has always given rise to conversation, so new media allow for ever more complex interaction between 'readers', or players, writers, and fans over the internet. These distinctions are interesting ones.

In his book *Cybertext: Perspectives on Ergodic Literature*, Espen Aarseth sets out to answer an apparently simple question which is whether computer games could be great literature. He also explores whether the rapidly changing genres of digital media are fundamentally reshaping our idea of what constitutes a story and the role the reader-player can assume. Is the dominant role of the narrative mode of discourse—that of novels, films, television and radio series—losing its position and influence in modern cultures? Do we now need to define, he asks, a new kind of aesthetics of 'cyborg textuality'. There are already a plethora of new media to consider in relation to reading. Take hypertext fiction. This uses links to allow the reader to chart his or her own progress through the story. The reader arranges a story from a wide range of possible configurations, constructing a story on the basis of only a fraction of the texts available from which to choose.

Yet European Modernist writers—James Joyce in *Ulysses* (1922), Jorge Luis Borges in *The Garden of Forking Paths* (1941), Italo Calvino in *The Castle of Crossed Destinies* (1973)—were already exploiting techniques that subverted the linearity of printed prose. The features of hypertext, including non-linearity, association, multipathing (a term borrowed from computing), are already present in Joyce's use of interior monologues which provide details which connect, sporadically, across the novel. This encourages a new kind of reading, one that often defies the prose's linearity and encourages instead a leafing backwards and forwards, even a skipping of sections of text. Readers are, in a sense, composing their own unique version of Joyce's enormous novel. The Choose Your Own Adventure series for young adults and other gamebooks of the same type are constructed along the same, if more limited, principles as cybertexts. *The Garden of Forking Paths* (1941) is an early and celebrated example.

Marc Saporta, *Composition* 1 (1962) is an early—if not the earliest—book in a box. The term is self-explanatory, except that it fails to explain that the 'book' is unbound. Each page contains a self-contained narrative fragment and it is the reader's job to assemble the pages into a 'book'. The reader may choose a few—or all—of the available pages.

Aarseth and others are also interested in the aesthetics and workings of digital literature, not just hypertext fiction, but also computer games, computer-generated fiction and poetry, and more recent innovations including collaboratively produced internet text-games, known as MUDs (Multi User Dungeons). Aarseth coined the term 'ergodic' to describe a reading process that required a different kind of effort from the reader from 'non-ergodic' texts. Instead of insisting on the fundamental newness of electronic and interactive reading modes, however, Aarseth draws our attention to the different ways in which the reader is expected to interact with the text. Guillaume Apollinaire's *Calligrammes* (1918), he points out, already require the reader to read in a new way in order to create a meaningful sequence. *Cybertext: Perspectives on Ergodic Literature* sees new electronic genres as part of a pre-digital tradition, denying the often-proposed and trenchant divide between the paper and the electronic, concluding, in relation to 'paper' stories: 'it is possible to explore, get lost, and discover secret paths in these texts, not metaphorically, but through the topological structures of the textual machinery.'

New media and new ideas for narrative which exploit their possibilities make new demands on readers. So too do new kinds of novels written along apparently conventional lines. Within the Anglo-American novel, for example, the recent burgeoning of the neurological novel is a case in point. Ian McEwan's *Enduring Love* (1997) is sometimes cited as one of the first and most accomplished. Jed, one of the characters in the novel, suffers from erotomania, or from the condition known as de Clerambault's syndrome, after the French psychiatrist of the same name. The condition is defined by the patient's delusional state, one in which he, or more commonly she, believes that someone considered to be of higher social and/or professional standing is in love with her. In addition, and quite as crucially, the novel is published with a case history, in an appendix, written by a fictional psychiatrist, and a bibliography. These addenda, which follow the novel proper, are, at the same time, part of it, but the reader is free to engage with them or not. But they imply that engaging with them will add to—or complete, possibly—the reading experience. Is the implication that we *need* some proper grasp of what this alleged psychiatric condition might be, in order to make proper sense of the novel?

Mark Haddon's *Curious Incident of the Dog in the Night-Time* is about a teenager with Asperger's syndrome, high-functioning autism, or savant syndrome, according to the book's cover. Haddon later denied that the book was 'about' Asperger's, writing, 'it's a novel about difference, about being an outsider, about seeing the world in a surprising and revealing way. The book is not specifically about any specific disorder.'

This genre of novel makes peculiar demands on the reader. This is in part because these novels are informed, to a greater or lesser extent, by new discoveries in neuroscience. But the backwards and forwards movement between the novel and what is discovered in other intellectual realms is surely another defining feature of the modern novel. In 1949, Lionel Trilling wrote, 'A specter haunts our culture—it is that people will eventually be unable to say, "They fell in love and married," let alone understand the language of *Romeo and Juliet*, but will as a matter of course say "Their libidinal impulses being reciprocal, they activated their individual erotic drives and integrated them within the same frame of reference."' Trilling was deriding what he saw as the reductive interpretations of human life proposed by Freudian and Jungian psychology, and its popular reinventions.

Today these explanations for our decisions, actions, and feelings have been largely replaced by neuroscientific accounts. We are familiar with endorphins, opiate receptors, and their analgesic effects, although whether or not we really understand the hormonal complexities of the biochemical makeups of our brains may be another matter. But the underlying anxiety Trilling diagnosed remains. We want to believe we are more than our brains. Are we? One of the reasons we continue to enjoy reading contemporary novels is that this is one of many compelling questions that they explore, because certain kinds of reading are above all a stimulus for our own minds. There is a tension or at least a spectrum associated with reading today. On the one hand there is a desire for the soundbite, for the meaningful fragment that conveys a great deal as economically as possible. On the other is the resilience of the literary text in all its richness of ambiguity. As Alan Bennett has Her Majesty the Queen declare at the end of his comic novella *The Uncommon Reader*: "'Briefing is not reading. In fact it is the antithesis of reading. Briefing is terse, factual and to the point. Reading is untidy, discursive and perpetually inviting. Briefing closes down a subject, reading opens it up."'

References

Chapter 1: What is reading?

Laqueur, Thomas, *Solitary Sex: A Cultural History of Masturbation* (Cambridge, Mass.: MIT Press, 2003).

Tschichold, Jan, *The Form of the Book: Essays on the Morality of Good Design* (Dublin: Hartley & Marks, 1991).

Rushdie, Salman, 'Notes on Writing and the Nation', *Index on Censorship*, vol. 26, no. 3 (1997).

Fischer, Steven Roger, *A History of Reading* (London: Reaktion Books, 2004).

Thrace, Arther S., *What Ivan Knows that Johnny Doesn't* (New York: Random House, 1961).

Coomaraswamy, Anada Kentish, *The Bugbear of Literacy* (Bedford: Perennial Books, 1979).

Chapter 2: Ancient worlds

Trimpi, Wesley, 'The Definition and Practice of Literary Studies', *New Literary History*, vol. 2, no. 1, *A Symposium on Literary History* (Autumn 1970).

Plato, trans. H. N. Fowler (London: Loeb Classical Library, 1913).

Finkelstein, David, and McCleery, Alistair, *An Introduction to Book History* (2nd edn, London and New York: Routledge, 2013).

Hackforth, R., *Plato's Phaedrus* (Cambridge: CUP, 1952, 2001).

Fischer, Steven Roger, *A History of Reading* (London: Reaktion Books, 2004).

Nietzsche, Friedrich, *Beyond Good and Evil*, trans. R. J. Hollingdale with an introduction by Michael Tanner (London: Penguin, 2003).

Fenton, James, 'Read my Lips', *The Guardian* (29 July 2006).

Balmer, Josephine (translator), *Sappho. Poems and Fragments* (Hexham: Bloodaxe Books, 2nd edn, 2018).

Chapter 3: Reading manuscripts, reading print

Brown-Grant, Rosalind, *Christine de Pizan and the Moral Defence of Women: Reading beyond Gender* (Cambridge: CUP, 1999).

Dittmar, Jeremiah E., 'Information Technology and Economic Change: The Impact of the Printing Press', *The Quarterly Journal of Economics*, vol. 126, no. 3 (August 2011).

McKitterick, David, *Print, Manuscript, and the Search for Order* (Cambridge: CUP, 2003).

Manguel, Alberto, *A History of Reading* (London: Flamingo, 1997).

Munday, Jeremy, *Introducing Translation Studies: Theories and Applications* (Abingdon: Routledge, 2001).

Smith, Helen, *Grossly Material Things: Women and Book Production in Early Modern England* (Oxford: OUP, 2012).

Kerby-Fulton, Kathryn, Thompson, John J., and Baechle, Sarah, *New Directions in Medieval Manuscript Studies and Reading Practices: Essays in Honour of Derek Pearsall* (Notre Dame, Ind.: University of Notre Dame Press, 2014).

Ginzburg, Carlo, *The Cheese and the Worms: The Cosmos of a Sixteenth Century Miller* (Baltimore: Johns Hopkins University, 1984).

Colclough, Stephen, *Consuming Texts: Readers and Reading Communities, 1695–1870* (Basingstoke: Palgrave Macmillan, 2007).

Chapter 4: Modern reading

Cavallo, Guglielmo, and Chartier, Roger (eds), *A History of Reading in the West*, trans. Lydia G. Cochrane (Oxford: Polity Press, 1999).

Roser, Max, 'Books'. Published online at OurWorldInData.org. (2017).

Attar, Samar, *The Vital Roots of European Enlightenment: Ibn Tufayl's Influence on Modern Western Thought* (Lanham, Md: Lexington Books, 2010).

Watt, Ian, *The Rise of the Novel: Studies in Defoe, Richardson and Fielding* (London: Penguin, 2015).

Jack, Belinda, 'Goethe's Werther and its Effects', *Lancet Psychiatry*, vol. 1, no. 1 (June 2014).

Darling, John, and Van De Pijpekamp, Maaike, 'Rousseau on the Education, Domination and Violation of Women', *British Journal of Educational Studies*, vol. 42, no. 2 (1994).

Schroder, Anne L., 'Going Public against the Academy in 1784: Mme de Genlis Speaks out on Gender Bias', *Eighteenth-Century Studies*, vol. 32, no. 3 (Spring 1999).

Jack, Belinda, *The Woman Reader* (London and New Haven: Yale University Press, 2012).

Barbauld, Anna Laetitia (ed.), *The Correspondence of Samuel Richardson*, vol. 6 (London: Richard Phillips, 1804; reprint New York: AMS Press, 1966).

Chapter 5: Forbidden reading

Fishburn, Matthew, *Burning Books* (Basingstoke: Palgrave Macmillan, 2008).

Nasifi, Azar, *Reading Lolita in Tehran: A Memoir in Books* (London: Fourth Estate, 2004; London: Penguin Classics, 2015).

Abanes, Richard, *Harry Potter and the Bible: The Menace behind the Magick* (Seattle, Wash.: Horizon Books, 2001).

Hill, Nathan, 'Harry Potter and Other Evils, or How to Read from the Right', *The Personalist Forum*, vol. 15, no. 2 (Fall 1999).

McDonald, Peter D., *The Literature Police: Apartheid Censorship and its Cultural Consequences* (Oxford: OUP, 2009).

Coetzee, J. M., *Giving Offense: Essays on Censorship* (Chicago and London: University of Chicago Press, 1996).

UNESCO, Institute of Statistics, Literacy.

Kirsop, Wallace, *Books for Colonial Readers: The Nineteenth-Century Australian Experience* (Melbourne: The Bibliographical Society of Australia and New Zealand in association with The Centre for Bibliographical and Textual Studies, Monash University, 1995).

Shattuck, Roger, *Forbidden Knowledge: From Prometheus to Pornography* (New York: St Martin's Press, 1996).

Potter, Rachel, *Obscene Modernism: Literary Censorship and Experiment 1900–1940* (Oxford: OUP, 2013).

Chapter 6: Making sense of reading

Weissbort, Daniel, and Eysteinsson, Ástráður, *Translation: Theory and Practice: A Historical Reader* (Oxford: OUP, 2006).

Allen, J. S., *In the Public Eye: A History of Reading in Modern France* (Princeton: Princeton University Press, 1992).

Jakobson, Roman, 'On Linguistic Aspects of Translation', in R. Brower (ed.), *On Translation* (Cambridge, Mass.: Harvard University Press, 1966).

Boase-Beier, J., Fawcett, A., and Wilson, P., *Literary Translation: Redrawing the Boundaries* (New York: Springer, 2014).

Weinberger, Eliot, and Paz, Octavio, *19 Ways of Looking at Wang Wei: How a Chinese Poem is Translated* (New York: Moyer Bell, 1987).

Kelleher, John V., 'The Perceptions of James Joyce', *The Atlantic Monthly* (March 1958).

Calvino, Italo, and McLaughlin, Martin (ed. and trans.), *Why Read the Classics?* (London: Penguin, 2009).

Lewis, C. S., *On Stories: And Other Essays on Literature* (New York: HarperCollins, 2017).

Barthes, Roland, *S/Z* (Paris: Éditions du Seuil, 1970).

Chapter 7: Pluralities

Aarseth, Espen J., *Cybertext: Perspectives on Ergodic Literature* (Baltimore: Johns Hopkins, 1997).

Further reading

Chapter 1: What is reading?

Coomaraswamy, Ananda Kentish, *The Bugbear of Literacy* (Bedford: Perennial Books, 1979).

Currey, James, *Africa Writes Back: The African Writers Series and the Launch of African Literature* (Oxford: James Currey, 2008).

Darnton, Robert, *A Case for Books: Past, Present and Future* (Philadelphia: Perseus Books, 2009).

Eliot, Simon, and Rose, Jonathan (eds), *A Companion to the History of the Book* (Oxford: Blackwell, 2009).

Fraser, Robert, *Book History Through Postcolonial Eyes: Rewriting the Script* (Abingdon and New York: Routledge, 2008).

Jack, Belinda, *The Woman Reader* (London and New Haven: Yale University Press, 2012).

Laqueur, Thomas, *Solitary Sex: A Cultural History of Masturbation* (Brooklyn: Zone Books, 2003).

Nord, David Paul, Rubin, Joan Shelley, and Schudson, Michael, *A History of the Book in America*, volume 5: 'The Enduring Book: Print Culture in Postwar America' (Chapel Hill, NC: The University of North Carolina, 2009).

Puchner, Martin, *The Written World: The Power of Stories to Shape People, History, Civilization* (New York: Random House, 2017).

SEAL website, Sources of Early Akkadian Literature.

Suarez, Michael, and Woudhuysen, H. R. (eds), *The Oxford Companion to the Book* (Oxford: OUP, 2010).

Chapter 2: Ancient worlds

Fischer, Steven, Roger, *A History of Reading* (London: Reaktion Books, 2004).

Gavrilov, A. K., 'Techniques of Reading in Classical Antiquity', *The Classical Quarterly*, vol. 47, no. 1 (1997).

Lyons, Martyn, *Books: A Living History* (London: Thames and Hudson, 2011).

Manguel, Alberto, *A History of Reading* (Canada: Vintage, 1998).

Chapter 3: Reading manuscripts, reading print

Eisenstein, Elizabeth L., *The Printing Revolution in Early Modern Europe* (Cambridge: CUP, 2013).

Febvre, Lucien, and Martin, Henri-Jean, *The Coming of the Book: The Impact of Printing 1450–1800* (London: New Left Books, 1976).

Gillespie, Alexandra, and Wakelin, Daniel, *The Production of Books in England 1350–1500* (Cambridge: CUP, 2011).

Ginzburg, Carlo, *The Cheese and the Worms: The Cosmos of a Sixteenth Century Miller* (Baltimore: Johns Hopkins University, 1984).

Kerby-Fulton, Kathryn, Thompson, John J., and Baechle, Sarah, *New Directions in Medieval Manuscript Studies and Reading Practices: Essays in Honour of Derek Pearsall* (Notre Dame, Ind.: University of Notre Dame Press, 2014).

McLuhan, Marshall, *The Gutenberg Galaxy: The Making of Typographical Man* (Toronto: University of Toronto Press, 1965).

Man, John, *The Gutenberg Revolution* (London: Review, 2002).

Smith, Helen, *Grossly Material Things: Women and Book Production in Early Modern England* (Oxford: OUP, 2012).

Chapter 4: Modern reading

Petroski, Henry, *The Book on the Shelf* (New York: Knopf, 1999).

Watt, Ian, *The Rise of the Novel: Studies in Defoe, Richardson and Fielding* (London: Penguin, 2015).

Chapter 5: Forbidden reading

Coetzee, J. M., *Giving Offense: Essays on Censorship* (Chicago and London: University of Chicago Press, 1996).

Croteau, David, Hoynes, William, and Hoynes, W. D., *The Business of Media: Corporate Media and the Public Interest* (Thousand Oaks, Calif.: Pine Forge Press, 2001).

Fish, Stanley, *There's No Such Thing as Free Speech … and it's a good thing too* (Oxford, OUP, 1994).

Fishburn, M., *Burning Books* (London: Palgrave Macmillan, 2008).

Kirsop, Wallace, *Books for Colonial Readers: The Nineteenth-Century Australian Experience* (Melbourne: The Bibliographical Society of Australia and New Zealand in association with The Centre for Bibliographical and Textual Studies, Monash University, 1995).

Lewy, Guenter, *Harmful and Undesirable* (Oxford: OUP, 2016).

McDonald, Peter D., *The Literature Police: Apartheid Censorship and its Cultural Consequences* (Oxford: OUP, 2009).

Moore, Nicole, *The Censor's Library* (Queensland: University of Queensland Press, 2012).

Morrison, Toni, *Burn This Book: Pen Writers Speak Out on the Power of the Word* (New York: Harper Collins, 2009).

Shattuck, Roger, *Forbidden Knowledge: From Prometheus to Pornography* (New York: St Martin's Press, 1996).

Tschichold, Jan, *The Form of the Book: Essays on the Morality of Good Design* (London: Lund Humphries, 1991).

Chapter 6: Making sense of reading

Boase-Beier, J., Fawcett, A., and Wilson, P., *Literary Translation: Redrawing the Boundaries* (New York: Springer, 2014).

Potter, Rachel, *Obscene Modernism: Literary Censorship and Experiment 1900–1940* (Oxford: OUP, 2013).

Weinberger, Eliot, and Paz, Octavio, *19 Ways of Looking at Wang Wei: How a Chinese Poem is Translated* (New York: Moyer Bell, 1987).

Weissbort, Daniel, and Eysteinsson, Ástráður, *Translation: Theory and Practice: A Historical Reader* (Oxford: OUP, 2006).

Chapter 7: Pluralities

Aarseth, Espen J., *Cybertext: Perspectives on Ergodic Literature* (Baltimore: Johns Hopkins, 1997).

Publisher's acknowledgements

We are grateful for permission to include the following copyright material in this book.

Extract from Anne L. Schroder. 'Going Public against the Academy in 1784: Mme de Genlis Speaks out on Gender Bias.' *Eighteenth-Century Studies*, vol. 32, no. 3 (1999): 376–82.

Extract from Sappho, translated by Josephine Balmer, *Sappho: Poems and Fragments* 2/e expanded (Bloodaxe Books, 2019). Reproduced with permission of Bloodaxe Books. <www.bloodaxebooks.com>.

Extract from *Chinese Lyricism*, by Burton Watson. Copyright © 1971 Columbia University Press. Reprinted with permission of the publisher.

The publisher and author have made every effort to trace and contact all copyright holders before publication. If notified, the publisher will be pleased to rectify any errors or omissions at the earliest opportunity.

Index

S

saccades 7
sacred texts 95–6
Saporta, Marc 116
Sappho 29
Sartre, Jean-Paul 102
Satanic Verses (Rushdie) 77, 83–4
scandal and gossip 32–3
scansion 13
Scott, Walter 53–4
self-censorship 92
Seneca 32–3, 81
Serbia, book burnings 79
Shaftesbury, Anthony Ashley-Cooper, 3rd Earl of 73–4
Shang civilization, China 15
Shattuck, Roger 93
Shikibu, Murasaki 56–7
silent reading 27, 36 *see also* reading aloud
social classes 49
Socrates 21, 24–6
Soliloquy, or Advice to an Author (Shaftesbury) 73–4
Sorrows of Young Werther, The (Goethe) 62–6
sounding out *see* phonics
South Africa
  banned books 86–7
  censorship 90
Soviet Union 19
  banned books 87–8
spans of recognition 7
speeches 97–8
state censorship 90–1
Strabo 29
Suetonius 32
suicide, influence of the novel 62–6
Sumerian accounting tablets 11–12
Swift, Jonathan 73

T

Tale of Genji (Shikibu) 56–7
Télémachus (Fénelon) 99–100
The Times newspaper 50
theology 15
Thucydides 26
Trace, Arther 19
translation 98
  of Arabic literature 57–8
  assassinations of translators 83–4
  of the Bible 44–5
  of German literature 64
  of Italian literature 70–1
  reservations about 100–1, 103–4
Tridentine Index 86
Trilling, Lionel 117–18
Trithemius, Johannes 40–1
Troth 24–5
Tschichold, Jan 5–7
Tyndale, William 78–9
typography 5–7

U

Uncommon Reader, The (Bennett) 118
understanding 5–7
United Nations, Universal Declaration of Human Rights 22
urban areas, vs. rural areas 51–2
urban expansion 50–1
Urban VIII, Pope 82–3
Uruk 12–13
Uruk (U-j) bone tags 11–12
USA 19
  American Library of Nazi Burned Books 80
  fundamentalists opposed to *Harry Potter* books 77, 85
  human rights 22
  literacy rates 52

SOCIAL MEDIA
Very Short Introduction

Join our community

www.oup.com/vsi

- Join us online at the official Very Short Introductions **Facebook** page.
- Access the thoughts and musings of our authors with our online **blog**.
- Sign up for our monthly **e-newsletter** to receive information on all new titles publishing that month.
- Browse the full range of Very Short Introductions online.
- Read **extracts** from the Introductions for free.
- If you are a teacher or lecturer you can order inspection copies quickly and simply via our website.

BESTSELLERS
A Very Short Introduction
John Sutherland

'I rejoice', said Doctor Johnson, 'to concur with the Common
Reader.' For the last century, the tastes and preferences of the
common reader have been reflected in the American and British
bestseller lists, and this *Very Short Introduction* takes an
engaging look through the lists to reveal what we have been
reading - and why. John Sutherland shows that bestseller lists
monitor one of the strongest pulses in modern literature and are
therefore worthy of serious study. Along the way, he lifts the lid on
the bestseller industry, examines what makes a book into a
bestseller, and asks what separates bestsellers from canonical
fiction.

> 'His amiable trawl through the history of popular books is frequently
> entertaining'

> **Scott Pack, The Times**

www.oup.com/vsi

BIOGRAPHY
A Very Short Introduction
Hermione Lee

Biography is one of the most popular, best-selling, and widely-read of literary genres. But why do certain people and historical events arouse so much interest? How can biographies be compared with history and works of fiction? Does a biography need to be true? Is it acceptable to omit or conceal things? Does the biographer need to personally know the subject? Must a biographer be subjective? In this *Very Short Introduction* Hermione Lee considers the cultural and historical background of different types of biographies, looking at the factors that affect biographers and whether there are different strategies, ethics, and principles required for writing about one person compared to another. She also considers contemporary biographical publications and considers what kind of 'lives' are the most popular and in demand.

'It would be hard to think of anyone better to provide a crisp contribution to OUP's Very Short Introductions.'

Kathryn Hughes, The Guardian

www.oup.com/vsi

CLASSICAL MYTHOLOGY
A Very Short Introduction
Helen Morales

From Zeus and Europa, to Diana, Pan, and Prometheus, the myths of ancient Greece and Rome seem to exert a timeless power over us. But what do those myths represent, and why are they so enduringly fascinating? This imaginative and stimulating *Very Short Introduction* is a wide-ranging account, examining how classical myths are used and understood in both high art and popular culture, taking the reader from the temples of Crete to skyscrapers in New York, and finding classical myths in a variety of unexpected places: from Arabic poetry and Hollywood films, to psychoanalysis, the bible, and New Age spiritualism.

www.oup.com/vsi

ENGLISH LITERATURE
A Very Short Introduction
Jonathan Bate

Sweeping across two millennia and every literary genre, acclaimed scholar and biographer Jonathan Bate provides a dazzling introduction to English Literature. The focus is wide, shifting from the birth of the novel and the brilliance of English comedy to the deep Englishness of landscape poetry and the ethnic diversity of Britain's Nobel literature laureates. It goes on to provide a more in-depth analysis, with close readings from an extraordinary scene in King Lear to a war poem by Carol Ann Duffy, and a series of striking examples of how literary texts change as they are transmitted from writer to reader.

{No reviews}

WRITING AND SCRIPT
A Very Short Introduction
Andrew Robinson

Without writing, there would be no records, no history, no
books, and no emails. Writing is an integral and essential part
of our lives; but when did it start? Why do we all write differently
and how did writing develop into what we use today? All of
these questions are answered in this *Very Short Introduction*.
Starting with the origins of writing five thousand years ago,
with cuneiform and Egyptian hieroglyphs, Andrew Robinson
explains how these early forms of writing developed into
hundreds of scripts including the Roman alphabet and the
Chinese characters.

'User-friendly survey.'

Steven Poole, The Guardian

www.oup.com/vsi